IT REVOLUTION IN ARCHITETTURA
series edited by Antonino Saggio

13

**EDIL**STAMPA
editrice dell'ANCE

SCIENTIFIC BOARD
Luca Galofaro
Domizia Mandolesi
Giuseppe Nannerini


COVER
*Manimal,* UnStudio

PHOTO CREDITS
Christian Richters, pp. 11, 12, 53, 56, 71, 74, 78, 88, 89, 90.
Iwan Baan, p. 57.
Other photographic images are courtesy of UnStudio

TRANSLATE FROM ITALIAN
Rebecca Guarda

LAYOUT
Pasquale Strazza


Edilstampa srl
Via Guattani, 24
00161 Roma
tel. 0684567403
fax 0644232981
www.edilstampa.ance.it

FIRST EDITION IN ITALIAN
Rome, November 2010

ENGLISH EDITION
Rome, October 2011

Andrea Sollazzo

# Digital Van Berkel
## Diagrams Processes Models of UNStudio

preface by Antonino Saggio

*For Riccardo*

*Ben Van Berkel and Caroline Bos at UNStudio, Amsterdam*

# Digital Sustainability

*preface by Antonino Saggio*

Without this rigorous management of the geometry, there would not have been such freedom in the architecture. Managing the mother model reduces the risks of mistakes and miscalculations; it helps to achieve an economy of materials, and makes the building process controllable. It is called digital sustainability.

*Ben Van Berkel*

The IT Revolution's reader is already familiar with the various frameworks of this book series. They can be analytical, expository or descriptive. Whenever the book title combines the word "digital" with the designer's name, the intent is to underscore that the architect, Van Berkel in this case, is exemplary in combining both an architectural design research with an original implementation of the field of Information Technology.

We have previously published volumes on the use of information technology in the works of Gehry (2001), Hadid (2004), Diller and Scofidio (2005) and Toyo Ito in 2008. *Digital van Berkel* now flanks these other volumes for it has achieved equally significant results in the international architectural scene, but with a noticeable difference from the architects mentioned above. Computer technology, for Ben Van Berkel and Caroline Bos, is a fundamental part of their architectural practice. Van Berkel and Bos also belong to a younger generation "born into the computer age" and, as such, their architectural research is permeated with this istrument. Let us try to understand how.

In the early nineties of the twentieth century, "Architectural Design" published *Folding Architecture*. The Magazine monographic issue was inspired by a Gilles Deleuze excerpt from his book *The Fold. Leibniz and the Baroque*. Folding is a design technique in which building components and the articulations of a landscape conform to one another via the act of bending. It is not the final form of the folding nor is it the bending itself that is interesting but, it is a more general approach that emerges, in which folding is simply an application.

A key word to address here is "diagram": an explanation of a series of relationships and possibilities existent within a project but that cannot be assimilated in the type or in the sketch. The diagram foretells "topological "and / or "parametric" relationships between the parts; (which simply means, that there exists an ample range of deformations that are "compatible" to the original). These concepts of mathematical derivation are of considerable relevance in the new computer age. The design process in architecture is a determination of relationships that create the final outcome. These relationships act as a sort of DNA code generator and control during the project development. The outcome depends on interventions that take place, as if they were variables, to evolve the diagram-code into one vs. another final design.

If Peter Eisenman is a reference for this design approach, as has often been written, then an important part of contemporary research is due to the logic of the diagram. Ben Van Berkel and Caroline Bos together created an original masterpiece that lucidly manifests the emerging power of diagrammatic reasoning.

The work is the Möbius House in Het Gooi designed and built in 1993-1999. The design shape is based on a diagram given by the famous Möbius ring: a solid line in the shape of ∞. Two entities, which in this case are a pair of intellectuals each with large zones for personal autonomy, are independent in some areas and intertwined in others. The design is elegantly resolved via the act of looping a planar ribbon about itself. UNStudio's economy of form as well as the powerful originality of the idea, creates a residential masterwork that is a key example of design through diagrammatic application.

If one compares the Esprit Nouveau pavilion of 1925 (Le Corbusier) and with the diagram constructed by Van Berkel and Bos at Het Gooi, one is immediately struck by the common course enthusiastically travelled by both. There exists the flat-planed box and production- assembly on the one hand, and the process flow-diagram of the computer on the other.

UNStudio is perhaps the most successful design team that is simultaneously in both the forefront of traditional architecture as well as in the world of digital research. This is why this book is so meaningful. The volume scans with an attentive eye the full body of work of the studio and interviews in depth Van Berkel, Bos and their design team. Sollazzo analyzes and understands the subject and then offers the reader, not airy critical interpretations, but a solid foundation on which to inquire, learn and apply their concepts. Digital sustainability is a key theme because the architects' design method relies heavily on computer technology. It is employed, not so much in terms of formal language but rather, for the computer modeling process as a critical component towards a changeable and interactive design that embraces a shifting flow of information.

The interaction and adaptability of computer modeling – the author writes – make the process of optimization smooth and uninterrupted: within a developed diagram one can swap, exchange and transform continuously the data and points of view, without in any way affecting its functionality and efficiency. It is essential to grasp that this is a revolution of the design process rather than in the design form. The dynamic of design is variable, cyclic and of process via: data entry – analysis - generation - testing – to then return to the upgrading of the equation with a new wave of updated data and targets in order to reach the required optimization. This explains another fundamental feature of the design model. Fluidity is not only understood at a formal level, but structurally the model must be open at any time towards updating and including new data from its very own fluid nature.

This book also brings me personal joy because I assisted the author in completing a long formative journey. He began in 1999 as a student of mine, developing significant work in a course on Terragni and followed this with a highly original thesis project.
Andrea Sollazzo lives and works in Rotterdam, and numbers among our group of architects that are – for various reasons (patronage, limited academic opportunity and a scarcity of employment options) – outside of Italy. I believe that within this author's writing and his solid comprehension of the implications of UNStudio's choices, lives an echo of our past work done in Italy. It is a pleasure to accompany this book with all that Edilstampa has created for us, printed and made available to a wide audience. *Digital UNStudio* by Andrea Sollazzo will not disappoint.

*www.arc1.uniroma1.it/saggio/IT/*

# 1. Organizational qualities of architecture

In the late eighties, we face the emergence of a new generation of architects and projects. The computer and Information Technology finally actively participate in the field of architecture, which renews itself and strives to keep up with what will become, from a technical, social and artistic standpoint, the cultural revolution of the century. The computer and the digital dimension are no longer theory, but become integral to the real world in which we operate. Since 1937, when the German scientist Konrad Zuse created and assembled the first mechanical binary calculator to drive Electric Z1, there has been an ever increasing integration in society of new information technologies. New models and parameters have developed, bringing about the birth of computer science, which, until the previous century, was non-existent. This new field has transformed the normal routine of daily life as well as our perception of time and distance. An overwhelming amount of knowledge, data, and information has been created and exchanged within a huge interactive network accessible to many. Society has become globalized with ever increasing layers of complexity, the capacity for abstraction has grown exponentially and the awareness of the difference between appearance and abstraction opens up endless fields of research; from physics to painting. Today's individual exists in multiple universes that simultaneously overlap and crowd each other. The digital world, our presence on the internet and electronic imprints today define a new and real dimension for the individual. This dimension often reveals completely new qualities, aspects and habits in our lives. Abstraction and exploration in all of the late twentieth and early twenty-first century arts show a general shift of interest from reproducing an interpretation of nature to an understanding of generative systems of a complex reality. For a product in a contemporary society, that already requires a high standard of performance, its attributed value is largely influenced by abstract information, messages, hints and suggestions. These abstractions subsequently create a qualitative classification of the object. The amount of research and information linked to an object manifestly and absolutely affects its value.

Amid this context, Ben Van Berkel trained at the Architectural Association in London while Caroline Bos attended Birbeck College, University of London, where she studied art history. They are among the first in Europe to focus on digital architecture as a research topic and to apply it methodically to the creative process as a tool for organization and for implementation. The awareness of society's current revolution and similar shift in the architectural field is momentous. Many of the concepts and processes of traditional architecture are being rewritten and the fundamentals of design have been shifting. It is not by chance that Ben Van Berkel, in explaining the impact of the digital age on architecture, uses concrete as a yardstick. That is to say that it was the introduction of new material that made possible the materialization of modern theories:

"... I am always very bold in affirming that the digital influence of the last sixteen - seventeen years in architecture has been as important to the profession as was the introduction of reinforced concrete. It began in the late nineties...".

As a first response to all this change, Van Berkel and Bos create a network of professionals ranging from architecture to engineering on through to botany, music and whichever skills the project requires. It is a flexible and branched network that better responds, compared to a traditional architectural team, to the contemporary needs for flexibility and complexity.

12  "We changed from van Berkel and Bos to UNStudio (United NetworkStudio) because we believed that the tradition of the architect's office was dull and did not work. Caroline and I are really advisors to the team. We discuss what we shall do with a particular location. I scribble and sketch, but then Caroline will come in and discuss how we program. It goes back and forth like this. Design comes very late with us." (Icon 2007, p... 117)

In project development, one is faced with an endless array of information and readily available data. It is a wealth of images, statistics, values, numbers, and stories; within the easy reach of any who inquire; to be taken, incorporated and multiplied. The modern city is a chaotic and layered organism that defines its identity through complexity and uncontrollability. The realm of the architect's daily task is to intervene in these complex organisms with applicable design structures and frameworks. It is more important to know how to filter information than to find and organize it. The true focus of the design is to distill this information. Architecture, in a city such as this, must go beyond traditional design theory,

ERASMUS BRUGGE,
ROTTERDAM, THE
NETHERLANDS, 1996
*Arial view and wireframe
computer model.*

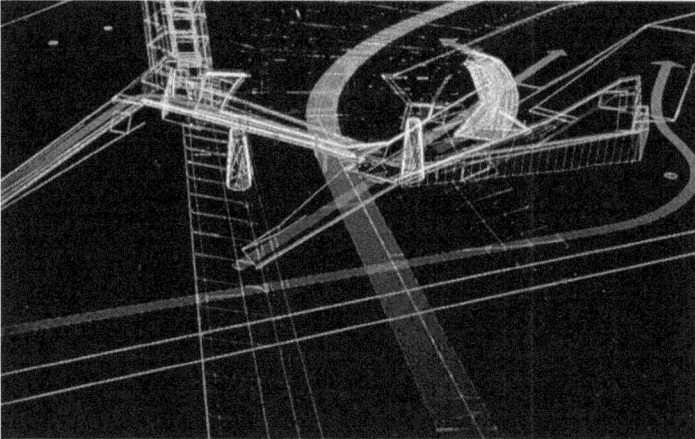

*UNStudio interior in Amsterdam.*

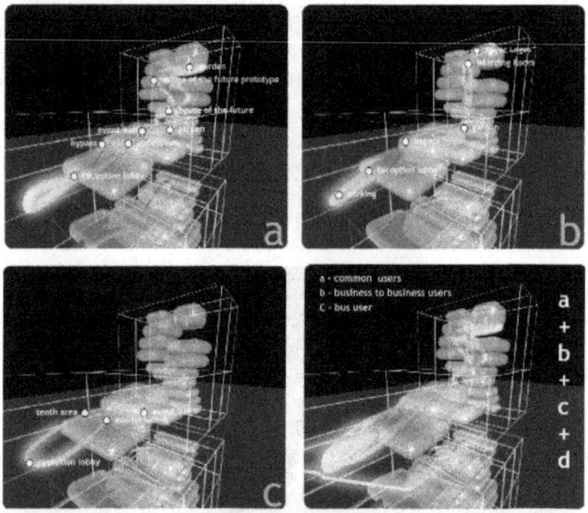

LIVING TOMORROW,
AMSTERDAM, THE
NETHERLANDS,
2000-2003

*Temporary pavilion designed and rendered in the studio for researching future housing using innovative technologies At center, Three-dimensional Diagrams; Below, Geometric reference model.*

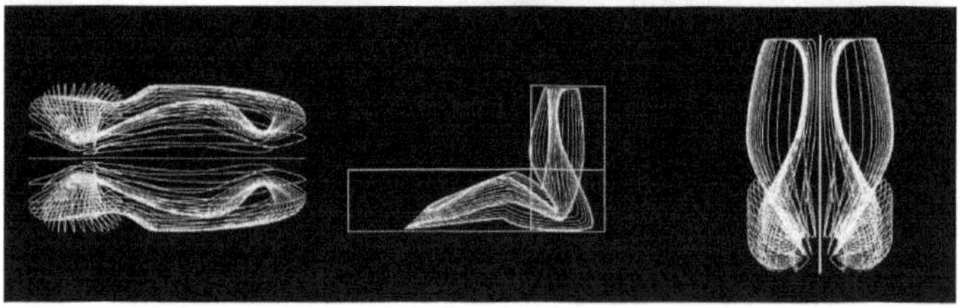

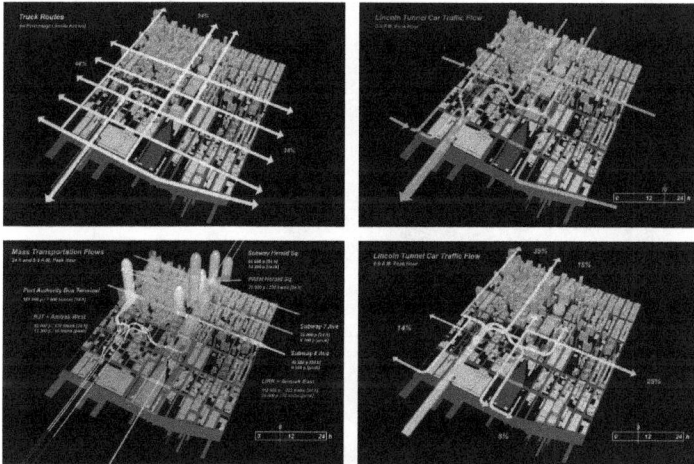

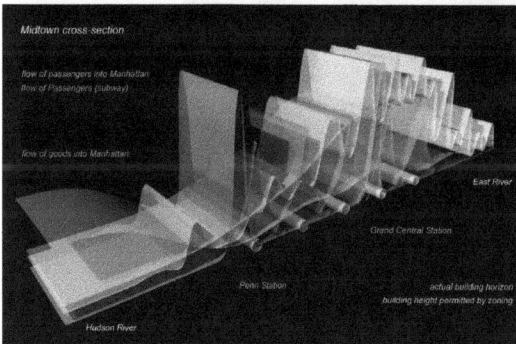

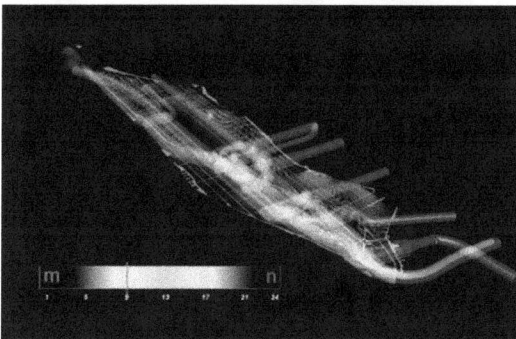

IFCCA, NEW YORK, USA, 1999

*Data and information is gathered and synthesized together with a time factor as well as with relevant moving components. Above, transportation system diagrams; Below, diagrams integrating the various program functions with a time factor.*

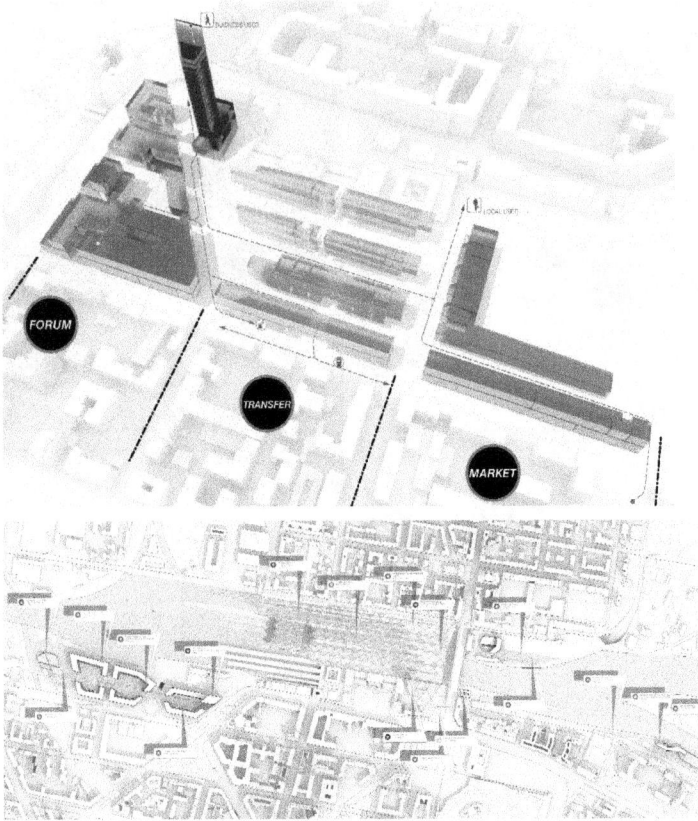

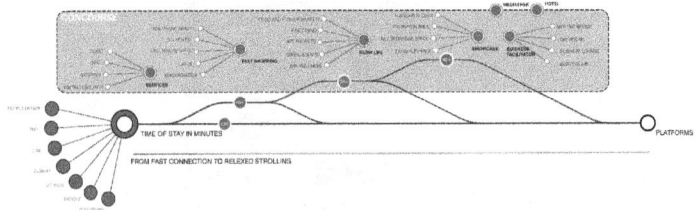

**BOLOGNA STATION, ITALY, 2007**

*Project for the design competition of a new railway station in Bologna. Master plan and diagrams: the great canopy system is the main architectural feature under which fluid and multiple activities are studied and organized.*

such as zoning or the concept of plain tray in order to be regarded as appropriate, and to contribute to the society's daily life and cultural development. Today the city is an organism that exists on multiple levels and simultaneously in multiple places. Contemporary cities are naturally interlinked, with shared infrastructures and it is not science fiction to speak of a fluid metropolis that breaks geographical boundaries. There is a need for architectural spaces that provide for all of this breadth while keeping up with the pace of our times. These spaces need to be symbols that stimulate this new city and help today's individual to better understand and live in real time. A shift of style becomes the typical established response, more or less successful, to this resulting design crisis.

## 1.1 Data

Let us start with what is currently the creative beginning and foundation of all architectural design: the accumulation of research data on a site, a program, a trademark, and anything that is going to affect the project. As mentioned before, today's data retrieval is available to everyone; the difference lies in the selection, management and interpretation of it. Architectural design can become a direct consequence of the accumulation and processing of data analysis, emerging from a new mentality, parametric, and the result of the opportunities given by the computer to organize, manage and display large amounts of data in relatively simple and immediate patterns. Deep Planning and Mobile Forces are terms introduced by Van Berkel and Bos for defining their approach. Their design methodologies anticipate a deep analysis of the context and the forces that develop in it as a starting point. Enormous attention is placed in the mapping of information relating to current and envisaged flows of movement which in turn, are integrated with dynamic time-sensitive data so as to arrive at defining the intended use. These types of analyses seek to integrate the individual within the program through the tracking of his movement. The difficulty in this approach is often how to define parameters that can describe complex situations such as those in the contemporary city. These parameters in UNStudio designs strive to centrally place the individual in the space and study his use of it over time. From this approach, they determine which are the vocations and the potentials of a given area.

| v-walls | cuts | kleinbottle | twist |

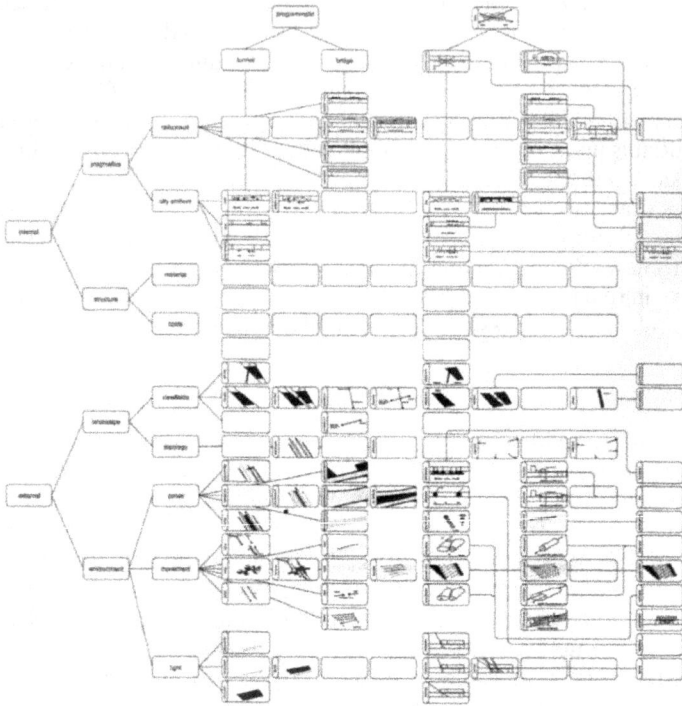

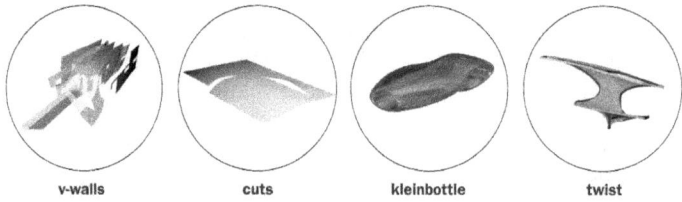

Conceptual tools

ARNHEM STATION, THE NETHERLANDS, 1996

"... it is an infrastructural hub that provides 160,000 square meters of mixed-use on a surface of 40,000 square meters and provides 6 different transport systems for a total of 55,000 passengers per week".

Organizational / formal matrix and various geometric patterns.

"Since no program is thinkable without people, no value can exist without users. Thus scanning a site for its flow structure shows up its real problems and potentials." (Van Berkel, P. Bos02. 38)

It is important to clarify that the computer and information technology come into play long before one begins to think about the definition of a form or geometry. These processes make up a new phase of the project that no longer bases the creative genesis through the suggestions of a sketch or a model. It is the formulation of a programmatic information schedule that defines a framework within which the project will come to life and find its place. UNStudio often measures itself against the field of urban planning; making larger urban infrastructure nodes one of the main 11, 13, 14 pillars of their research. This is evident in projects such as IFFCA in New York, the Erasmus Bridge in Rotterdam, the Ponte Parodi in Genoa and in the Bologna railway station. The amount of data, information and influences in the site is so broad and complex that it can hardly be extracted and synthesized without the use of the computer. The design for the Arnhem train station is an infrastructural hub that provides 160,000 square meters of mixed-use on a surface of 40,000 square meters and provides 6 different tran- 16, 18, 19 sport systems for a total of 55,000 passengers per week. All this must be combined at the end of the design process into a coordination of structures that exist both as symbolic and emotive identities of a train station. The design acts as a place of departure and arrival, as well as symbol of a city whose life continues throughout the day and night. It is often believed that approaches like this one will lead to an architecture where the architects become deterministic and avoid their responsibilities by hiding behind a blind faith in digital and computer science as infallible systems of design and analysis.

However, architecture brings forth other abstract fundamental values, which are incorporated from the beginning. In fact, if it is true that the amount of data and its availability is no longer an obstacle, then the attention and responsibility shifts to the which data to analyze and how to relate its components with each other. This brings the architect to the crucial role of selection and management. Within the "what-if" approach, the end result is closely related to the selection of input data: the phase of research, analysis and data processing is already a critical step despite being abstract

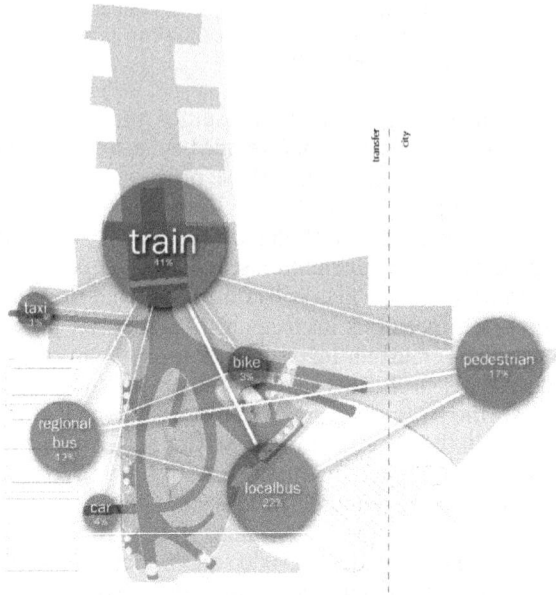

ARNHEM STATION, THE NETHERLANDS, 1996

*Placement and connections of the various transport systems and rendering of the station looking from the square in front of the main entrance.*

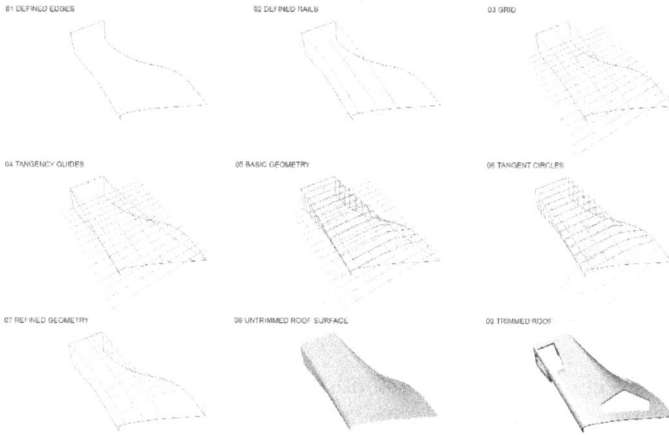

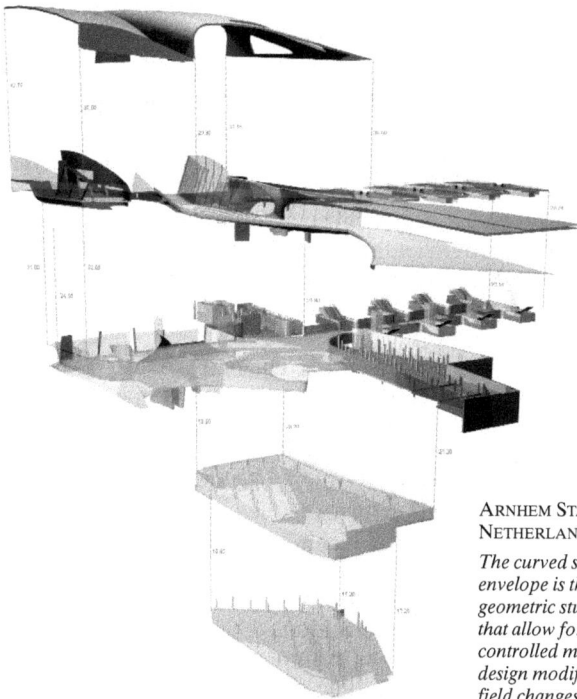

ARNHEM STATION, THE
NETHERLANDS, 1996

*The curved surface of the
envelope is the product of
geometric studies
that allow for the
controlled management of
design modifications and
field changes.*

and unrelated to any formal vision, planning and design development. Data and statistics are silent regulators which, via their in-
terconnection and interaction, speak to us in varying degrees. Van
Berkel and Bos put much emphasis on the concept of Deep Planning as a method to generate a potential design that is based on in-
terrelationships of data as opposed to individual components.

13, 16   "[...] as a result, relations instead of the optimization of individual data from
the parameters of the projects, generating potentials that no single, individual
interest could have generated.... The Deep Plan offers a new abstraction
which, unlike the reductionism of an urbanism based on Euclidean geometry,
is proliferating, unfolding and generative, reactivating public life in urban
planning." (Van Berkel, Bos 2008, p. 32).

The selection of data and methods in which to correlate the givens
becomes the architect's exclusive responsibility.

*1.2 The calm after the storm: a bazaar of forms*

Van Berkel and Bos, by their own admission, have always been extremely interested in the developments of digital culture in architecture and in the formal and procedural changes the design field
has undergone. Perhaps it is precisely because of this factor that
the analysis phase in today's architectural field has become so lu-
cid and straightforward. The enormous enthusiasm for and propa-
gation of digital creativity of the nineties, is undergoing a new phase. UNStudio, NOX, their Dutch counterpart, as well as Gehry, Li-
beskind, Eisenman and Hadid, to name a few of the famous designers of the nineties, were finally able to liberate their vision,
thanks to the computer. This vehicle enabled them to place emphasis on creative flow with revolutionary epoch-making results
that undoubtedly gave the designers an unprecedented free reign
in the conceptual research of spatial design. However, in today's
second phase, the ease of access to 3D modeling techniques and
the facilitation of production have enabled hyper-creative formalism with a virtuosity of digital technology that rarely engages se-
rious spatial research with programmatic, urban and conceptual
functions. Our alleged contemporary symbols, from Dubai to the
mega-structures of various international exhibitions including the
Olympic Games are an obvious example of this. The market's de-
mand for novelty, for the building of icons and for the public's

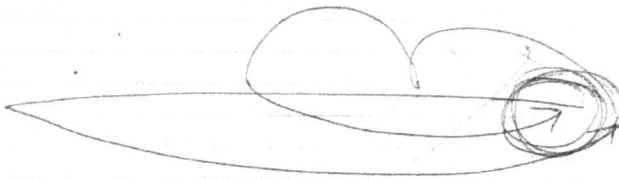

*"In the end, all these forms and antics do nothing but accumulate and settle into a sort of virtual bazaar of strange and extreme shapes in which they all end up similar to one another".*
*Above: OMA, Renaissance tower, Dubai, collage. Center: Dubai, formal bazaar, Aerial photograph of the skyline. Below: the extension of the line (B. Van Berkel).*
*"Huge leaps were made in the dark and ideas were launched of which the consequences were ignored. The subject of debate has shifted, almost unconsciously, beyond the established limits. We have moved beyond".*

amazement leads to a vacuous creation of urban scale gimmicks that have little to do with architecture. Any student today can easily design bizarre and astonishing skyscrapers and any team of engineers can transform them into buildings. In the end, all these forms and antics do nothing but accumulate and settle into a sort of virtual bazaar of strange and extreme shapes that all end up similar to one another.

21 Unregulated and complicated forms have become obvious today. All kinds of Blob Architecture are becoming too wild and too similar to itself. Everybody today makes Blob Architecture so, I wonder, what makes it so special? I believe that if we are not careful, all this will become a big bazaar of free-style shapes, and I honestly believe that if we are not able to carefully formulate what we do with the computer and a digital discipline of architecture, then we are losing the fundamental principles and methods by which design tools in architecture have always been used. (Van Berkel 09)

The practice of creating something strange and astonishing, at any cost, has led to a dangerous stagnation in the architectural revolution of the nineties. Van Berkel and Bos are absolutely aware of this risk and number among the first to make a conscious attempt to stop and think about what it means to practice digital design architecture after the past ten years. A deep reflection is essential and many parameters and assumptions must be refined and reformulated. The call to discipline and for digital consciousness is fundamental in order for the revolutionary process not to run aground. Like all revolutions, it begins alive with passion and enthusiasm, but must become structured, with rules and schedules in order not to lose its impact. Nothing is denied, but one analyzes after the fact and tries to streamline and understand the process, which guided by intuition and by talent has helped stretch boundaries in the past and opened up unexplored fields. Huge leaps were made in the dark and ideas were launched of which the consequences were ignored. The subject of debate has shifted, almost unconsciously, beyond the established limits. We have moved beyond. Now is the time to grasp what was behind those acts and operations. One must understand and structure these new fields to make them fertile and solid ground on which to build our new forms of contemporary architecture. The moment for provocation has passed and a need for structure and discipline has arisen. We must understand and differentiate what is real and important from

past research and what we can dismiss as a mere fad with superficial enthusiasm.
The return to discipline, to a digital discipline is a fundamental thesis in UNStudio's work. They equally focus on what it means to think digitally and on what the added value of computer use can be on the architectural program of use, the physical materiality and the interrelating of new architectural and urban spaces.

I like to be considered an experimental architect who broadens the possibilities of the organization of architecture; UNStudio is also related to this idea of endless re-organization. [...] I am interested in this organizational quality in architecture. (Van Berkel 09)

UNStudio research departs from this platform and it is from this standpoint that one must understand the importance of Van Berkel and Bos' work. Today, even more than in the past fifteen years, we are in need of computer theory and discipline. The limitless ideas and visions launched by modernist architecture were the right and necessary ones to access new frontiers. Today's UNStudio tries to synthesize within a clear framework all the required and intuitive operations with formal, programmatic and methodological innovations that clear the field of dangerous misunderstandings and inconsistent tendencies.
UNStudio's design basis consists of three fundamental:
- design models
- digital thinking
- the programmatic requirements of architectural design

# 2. Principles for digital design and computer architecture

*2.1 Design models: dynamic and transformative models*

By taking the best from contemporary challenges and stimuli, UNStudio sets in motion a complete rethinking of the design process. They search for a quick, concise and effective response to ever-changing issues and problems that are well documented and archived in databases. A tool is needed; a response that makes the final leap in design, that is able to trigger the complex processes, which involve multiple disciplines and points of view, to achieve a modern and viable end product. The correlation of data proves imperative. The UNStudio creative process offers an innovative methodology. Their process triggers a series of oscillations that define the project in a circular manner typical of combinatorial computer techniques rather than the modernist tradition for a linear process of Euclidean geometry and design sequencing. It is against this backdrop that the fundamental and indispensable role of the diagram emerges as the basic tool for creating and managing it. The diagram is the trigger that activates the generative process and, at the same time, defines rules, margins, proportions, influences and dimensions. It acts as the bridge between the abstract and the material. This tool conceptually transforms ever changing information into an aesthetic, communication, a summary and a generator.

Among the Dutch, the design use of the diagram is certainly not exclusive to UNStudio. Rem Koolhaas is foremost in choosing the diagrammatic approach as a key player in the representation of contemporary architecture. What distinguishes the UNStudio diagrams is their clear and immediate connection to information technology and digital imaging: their diagrams are generated on the computer, with the computer, for the computer. The interactivity and adaptability of computer modeling makes for a fluid and continuous process of optimization: It is possible, within a well-designed diagram, to continuously exchange, vary, and modify data and points of view without altering its functionality or effectiveness. It is important to understand that this is a revolution of design process rather than of form. The design process is fluid, cyclic, one that proceeds via: - data entry - analysis - generation - te-

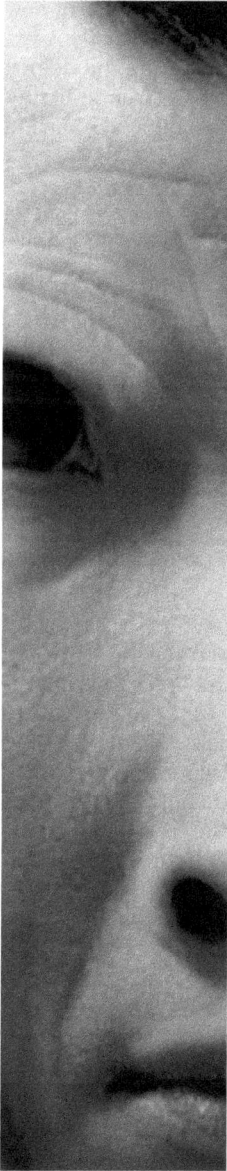

MANIMAL, UNSTUDIO

*Digitally rendered image. Morphing of man/dog/serpent. The boundaries between the various elements become unrecognizable. The resultant creation is a new image that is no longer the superimposition of different images.*
*Below: F. Picabia, 1958, collage, Madame Picabia.*

sting - to then return and update the equation with a wave of new data targeted toward the required optimization level. This explains another fundamental characteristic of computer modeling, its fluidity not exclusive to formalism, but key to a structural integrity of the model: it must be open at all times to the updating and inclusion of data that by its very own nature is in flux.

"This endless fluctuation, which forms a dizzying structure composed of counteracting and interlocking flows, represents perhaps the only possible foundation for an architecture of *InFormation*." (Bos95, p... 98)

The uniqueness of the diagram is its being in the middle, in its being a bridge and a springboard, in its being able to give applied answers to abstract values. It is an abstraction with three-dimensional, geometric and architectural values.

"Diagrams operate as abstract machines for proliferation; they are generative; they incorporate specific information; and they unfold in their complexity. Van Berkel breathes new life into abstraction, functionalism and formalism by using abstraction in a generative rather than reductive manner." (Lynn95, p. 31).

Although in some ways atypical, Manimal is a concise graphic re-
25 presentation of a face created by *Morphing*, i.e. the digital fusion of three different living beings: man, snake and horse. It is important precisely because of its diagrammatic value. The image represents in a graphic, precise, real and tangible manner all the qualities of mediation, interaction, communication and abstraction of an actual design model. The interaction between the input data, the value that is associated with it and the final result is more evident than ever here. There exists a shift in the balance between the three entities in regards to the consequential greater likelihood of one the three undermining and disrupting the image of a synthesized hybrid; the goal of the entire experiment. This creature *of the middle* is difficult to categorize according to classical typologies. It is the perfect symbol of mediation and transformation traditional to UNStudio. Creating form alone is not enough but rather, the resultant form is a creative and effective response to the demands of the contemporary world, a new image, a digital image.
25 Manimal sums up complexity: it is the digital solution to collage,

which modernism previously exalted as the vehicle for highlighting overlaps, conflicts and tensions of a culture and of a Cartesian-based model. The focus, however, shifts in Manimal to the contact point between the different elements to the point of fusion. It transcends the collage. One can no longer perceive outlines of the individual identities that make up the character; creating tensions interior to the image and enriching the reading of its sources.

Instrumental to this effect are the use of digital and interactive imaging techniques, design and organization via layers and hierarchies, and the use of animation in which the time factor can be actively integrated.

Different professional disciplines and approaches array themselves around the diagram. The diagram becomes a communal palimpsest, understood by all because its rule-based graphics remain simple, yet inclusive of all necessary information; and a constant point of reference providing coherence and discipline to the project.

Computer design models can be used, for example, to select choices consistent with the needs of a building. They can function as prototypical principles; you can filter the project so that you do not disperse in all directions. And this is what worries me. Because of the computer, architecture is becoming more and more homogeneous; buildings become more irrational; the irrationality is always the same wherever you look. There is no longer a discipline in today's formalism. Design models can help you find this discipline. (Van Berkel 09) [21]

Reflecting on what Betsky states about the importance of this case (Betsky, 2002, p. 7), it is important to clarify that UNStudio does not undermine the look or content of their projects with simple eye-catching aesthetics. Thanks to their use of diagrammatic design models, they interrelate content with form and maintain a formal and conceptual coherence that creates a quality product both in terms of aesthetic and content. The discipline mentioned by Van Berkel is employed precisely to ensure that the limitless formal potential provided by modern technologies does not become the focus of their research.

## 2.2 The design model is the tool, but never the design itself

It is important to understand this and it is an essential pillar to avoid collapse. The architect 's efforts must not be misdirected into the designing of overly complex models, scripts, and project management systems that often prove useful only to themselves. The scale of the diagram should be both intuitive and applicable to the design problem.

The call to discipline, a digital discipline is a recurring theme of UNStudio today: their 2006 publication of *Design Models* is a key source towards understanding their work. The various design models created over the years by the studio, are categorized and regrouped into five main interconnected families (inclusive principle, mathematical model, V model, Blob to Box model and the principle of Deep Planning - see Glossary).

The publication explains and illustrates in depth their use of the diagram in both the design and construction of architecture. The vital connections and relationships in the digital discipline between the design and the computer model are explained and rationalized, often in retrospect. The designers are often initially unaware of the depth of these original links. They come to realize that many of the previous design moves were much more complex than expected and they attempt to use this complexity to form a solid and creative paradigm within which to proceed without further confusion. The studio strives to provide an amniotic fluid in which the new digital architecture, even as it incubates, may grow as much as possible in a "healthy" and "balanced" manner. The interaction between different models internal to the design is a cross-section that produces a final result with no semblance to the original design. This fruit is born of a deliberately complex and chaotic design process, which does not follow rationalist linear sequencing.

"It is not a literal following [of the model]. That does not interest me. We need a main guiding principle. I am more interested in the instrumentalization of the model and of the diagram, and in the way you can use process [in design]. I am not interested in literal representation of the model." (Van Berkel 09)

The digital model is created simultaneous to a project's design, in response to specific research to then be applied again in other

*Image from "Move", UNStudio, 2008: summary diagram of the different design models applied to the projects.*

*The projects are not literal translations of a single model, but the result of a critical and innovative development of the five basic design principles defined by UNStudio. The overlapping and combination of different models multiply indefinitely the design possibilities, while maintaining a steady overarching criterion for developing the project. Icons of project models: 1. Deep Planning 2. Inclusive Principle 3. V Model 4. Mathematical Model 5. Blob-to-Box*

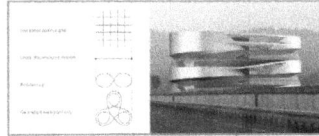

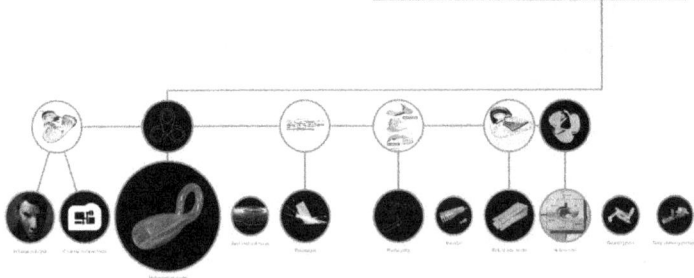

MERCEDES BENZ MUSEUM, STOCKEM, GERMANY, 2001-2006
*Integration of different referenced design models.*

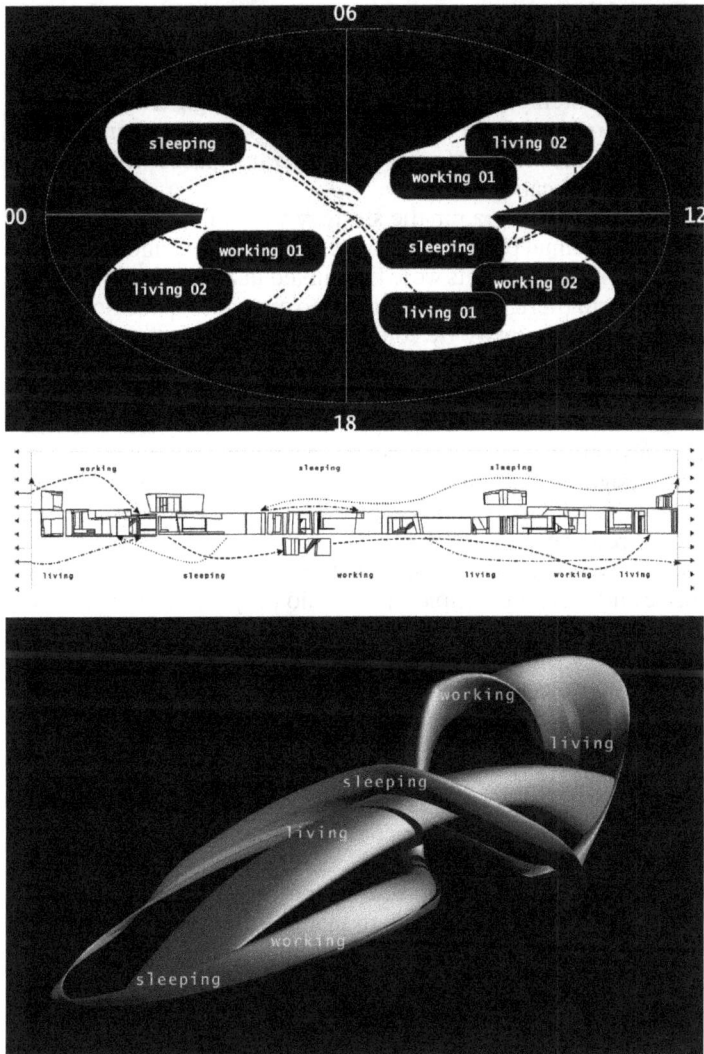

MOBIUS HOUSE, HET GOOI, THE NETHERLANDS, 1993-1998

*Formal and programmatic diagrams: "A formal and programmatic strategy was followed, referencing the four cardinal points, to connect them in a fluid and interesting manner".*

project designs and be transformed therein with new values and
31 potential. For example, the model of Möbius ribbon, born from
the Möbius house design, is added to UNStudio's shared vocabulary for contemporary architecture. The design criteria for the
Möbius house came from wanting to integrate the program of use
with an interrelation of residential private spaces with a varied
and rich landscape.

A formal and programmatic strategy was followed, referencing
the four cardinal points, to connect them in a fluid and interesting
manner. The four points were first linked in a traditional linear fashion. From there, UNStudio strove to make the space richer with
increasing complexity by combining the different points of the
house in a non-linear fashion. The cardinal points were interlaced
and, at this point, the Möbius ribbon revealed itself as the perfect
synthesis of this move. This approach of continuity and complexity in a single gesture can equally be found in *Manimal*.

The design model organizes a series of principles: it works as a
prototype, which generates related projects that are designed and
cross-bred using different model types. The final designs bear no
visual resemblance, but share consistent organizational, programmatic and formal principles. UNStudio projects are mostly easily
29 grouped into families. An interchangeable fluidity is not only internal to a specific project, but can be traced conceptually from
34,35 project to project. The St. Petersburg Dance Palace is the most re-
cent work, and certainly not definitive, of a series of public buildings that posit a number of concepts and a common architectonic language.

33 UNStudio projects such as the Spijkenisse theatre, the Audito-
56,57,88 rium of Padova, or the Agora theater rather than the one of Graz
apply the "inclusive principle" models as a key players in the design phase such as the Blob-to-box or other mathematical models
to filter in a natural and smooth manner the transition from city
to the magic world of theater. The variety of programmatic space
in the theatre complexes, with associated formal and technical requirements, is bridged with the city via a powerful public thre-
shold of retail and gathering spaces. The foyer and the facade become the melting point of city and theatre. They simultaneously
provide a formal and programmatic gravitational center for the
project. Architectural design is no longer seen as the search for
the unique work of art, but it is an ongoing dialogue in a vital re-

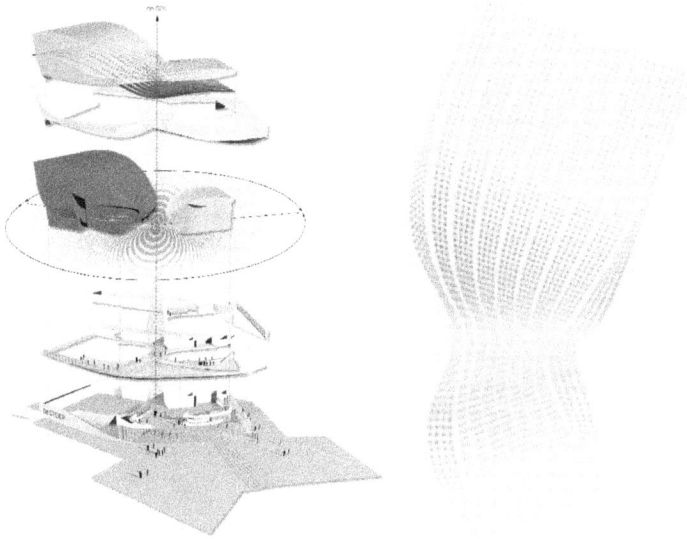

SPIJKENISSE THEATER, THE NETHERLANDS, 2008

*Extruded perspective and skin pattern. The density of openings corresponds to the transition from public to private spaces.*

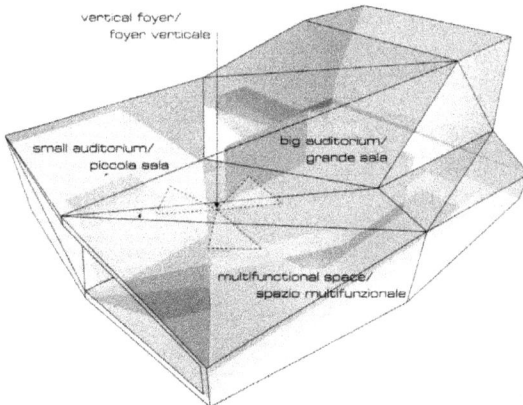

AGORA THEATRE, LELYSTAD, THE NETHERLANDS, 2007

*The external volume wraps the different rooms of the theater adapting and following the different programmatic needs.*

**DANCE PALACE, SAINT PETERSBURG, RUSSIA, 2009**

*Diagram guide.
The interaction with the site and the city represents the forces that shape the volume of the theater. The envelope itself and facades become modeled in relation to the program of use.*

гибкая Х-модель
FLEXIBLE X-TYPE

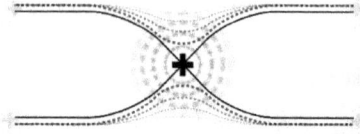

Поворотный момент
Pivotal Point

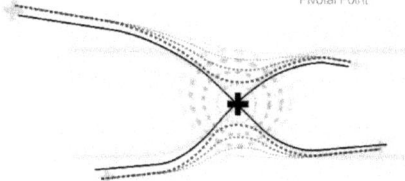

Смещение пунктов назначения
Distorted Target Points

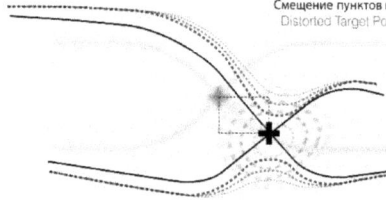

Сдвиг поворотного момента
Shifted Pivot Point

Принцип плана
PLAN PRINCIPLE

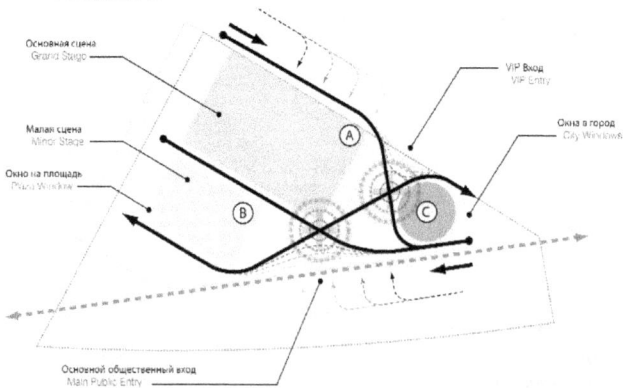

Основная сцена
Grand Stage

Малая сцена
Minor Stage

Окно на площадь
Plaza Windows

VIP Вход
VIP Entry

Окна в город
City Windows

Основной общественный вход
Main Public Entry

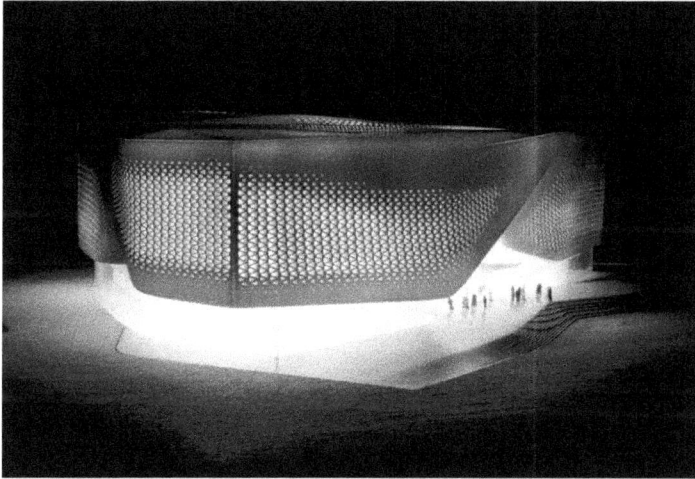

DANCE PALACE, SAINT PETERSBURG, RUSSIA, 2009
*Model, rendering e aerial perspective.*

search field that is open for development and enrichment. Each individual work should not be analyzed as a separate end in itself, but should be contextualized within a wider, complex research that is linked project-to-project. UNStudio's urban scale projects are another example of this approach. For scheduling reasons, the studio developed these projects simultaneously such as the IFCCA New York, the Harnem Station, or Ponte Parodi in Genoa.

The research themes here are similar, and make up part of their Deep Planning studies. These studies explore how to read and analyze vital aspects and patterns of a city and how to synthesize and apply this data in programs and forms within a prototype and maintain a broad and rigorous discipline

"I call these 'design models'. They require a prototypical way of thinking: you have one prototype and from here you can develop other kinds of designs. What is interesting about this is that you have a particular formal repetition and it organizes any complexity in a serial way of disciplining a geometrical partition." (Van Berkel 09)


*2.3 Digital thinking*

UNStudio maintain their focus on defining what digital actually means and what digital thought may be. What is digital? What has it changed? And in what way? What new areas and what unknowns has computer aided design brought to architecture? To understand this, they question what the concrete changes are today and what may still change in relation to past architecture. They strive to uncover the essence of contemporary society and architecture; constantly questioning the why and the real meanings of actions, what are real discoveries and what are simply passing blunders.

The role of UNStudio is very similar to that of the scientist, who researches, experiments and tries to uncover new ways and possibilities based on ever evolving knowledge and techniques. Innovation, new areas and problems posed by the advent of computers and of digital culture, are debated with the spirit and enthusiasm of the scientist. Intrigued and stimulated, they attempt to look into an existing system and generate something new and useful. These systems, that seem abstract speculations, are often real conceptual leaps that open up infinite new challenges and issues. They challenge the axis of the balance and require a response and reformulation of the "architectural universe."

## 2.4 Rubber Mat

The city of Rotterdam commissioned UNStudio in 1995 to perform a study of potential urban and architectural developments of specific areas of the city over the next 50 years. The studio found itself facing a very complex and open-ended design problem such as foreseeing the city's future growth in both urban and architectural scales.

This is an innovative work by UNStudio and anticipates by a decade technical approaches that, in the course of the twenty-first century's early years, will become common practice in urban research and planning. Van Berkel and Bos are aware of the futility of predicting and planning a futuristic architectural form for the city. They let go of guessing the formal and aesthetic aspect of the research and focus instead on the design of a functional model for future growth.

"The computerized organizational model of the Rubber Mat avoids architecture; the Rubber Mat constitutes an early version of an aesthetically neutral futurological instrument." (Van Berkel, Bos 08, page. 472)

They present an original and innovative approach that is far from any other proposal or projection to date that focuses on architectural and material forms.

The imaginary city of the future with flying cars and mega infrastructure is not drawn; as was done by Le Corbusier and proposed by Archigram. Rubber Mat analyzes the system of forces that [38] move and shape the city. It proposes an abstract and functional model that materializes these forces together with a recurrent theme of interactivity and adaptability.

Four conditions of the city are analyzed: living, work, fun and the landscape that are tracked on a horizontal timeline within a [39,40] three-dimensional model that has the shape of the city. These are contrasted with parameters that modify the four different layers along a vertical line. These parameters are: the land value, rent level, building density, occupational density, increase in business activities, in services and in landscape quality. Any changes in these parameters will affect four different conditions. This creates a

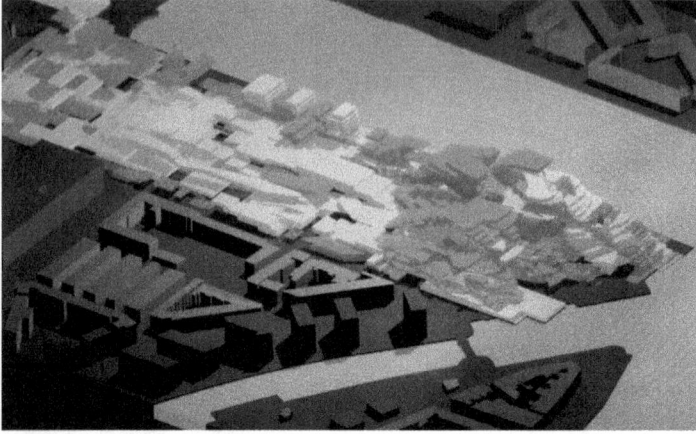

RUBBER MAT, ROTTERDAM, THE NETHERLANDS, 1995

*Three-dimensional image of the digital analysis and development model for the urban renewal of South Rotterdam. "The imaginary city of the future with flying cars and mega infrastructure is not drawn; as was done by Le Corbusier and proposed by Archigram."*

*Le Corbusier, new plan for Algiers, 1929.*

*Archigram, A Walking City, England, 1964.*

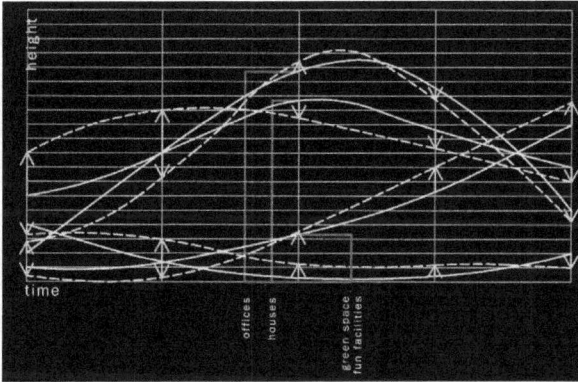

*Diagram interrelating the five parameters (the land value, rent level, building density, occupational density, increase in business activities, in services and in landscape quality) with the time factor.*

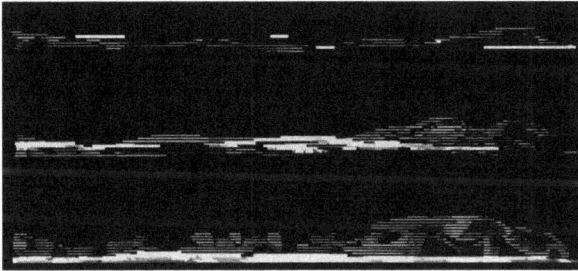

*Phases development: evolution in time of the four analyzed conditions: living, working, fun and landscape*

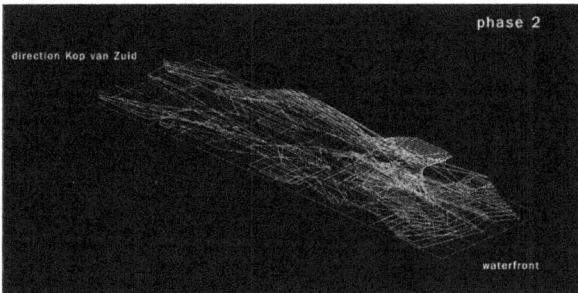

*3dimensional wireframe visualization of the evolution phase 2*

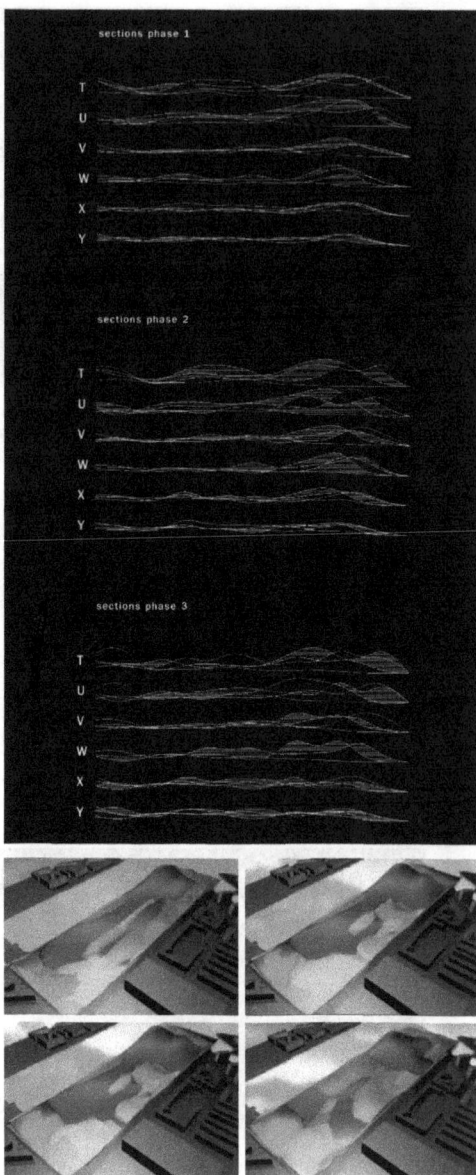

sections phase 1

T
U
V
W
X
Y

sections phase 2

T
U
V
W
X
Y

sections phase 3

T
U
V
W
X
Y

Rubber Mat,
Rotterdam, The
Netherlands, 1995

*Different stages of
model development:
sections and three-
dimensional color
diagrams. The four
schemes and associated
color diagrams are
interrelated by a series
of interdependent links
and factors.
In this model, as in any
urban context, the
different components of
the city must not be
considered in isolation.
Each design move on a
specific sector activates
a series of rippling
effects on neighboring
components within the
greater organism. This
type of model does not
represent the physical
shape of the city, but
images existing
economic, social and
environmental
relationships. (Deep
Planning). The city is a
dynamic organism and
as such represents an
intersection of forces
and parameters that are
either directly or
indirectly linked.*

sort of "water bed" (according to van Berkel), where a pressure is [40] generated in a reaction to others. These changes are then integrated with the equation of time charting and materializing possible transformations of the zone, always keeping the different forces in relation to the different research parameters. The result is a clear example of *ante litteram* parametric techniques applied to the study of cities and to architecture.

Processes such as these, which are now beginning to become commonly used, had not yet been applied at the time of the project and show that, even before the intervention of computer tools, such types of development analysis and parametric thinking, was already present in UNStudio's digital architecture and urban design. They saw the city not so much as a mere collection of buildings and forms, but as a system and set of forces and values that can be, thanks to a new mindset and new tools, systematized in to a design model, that can forecast and be simultaneously interactive and pragmatic.

Even after fifteen years, this type of research remains applicable and innovative and has not yet reached a concrete materialization and realization in the field. The idea remains ahead of what is commonly practiced and there exist research and development fields introduced by information technology still to be developed and fully applied. Approaches such as these truly change the substance of the process and introduce a completely new way of thinking and organizing the architecture of the city. UNStudio's work seeks to understand and analyze the forces that hide beneath the surface of the city. They are interested in the abstract principles that organize the city and the relationships and connections that exist between them. Obviously it is an extremely complex research problem, far more complex than simply generating breathtaking futuristic forms. The real challenge lies in reformulating the principles of organization, spatiality and design of architecture.

## 2.5 The expansion of the line

UNStudio's analysis and proposals revolve around the ideas of scope, boundary, organization, system, method and substance.

"[Today] we are able to expand the modernist model, make it longer and stretch it out. I think we have not yet developed a very strong theory about this aspect of the digital. With the digital we are able to stretch the possibili-

ty of architecture, on both sides, towards the aesthetic and towards the idea of
efficiency. Efficiency today is the word for functionality." (Van Berkel 09)

UNStudio focuses on what the information technology revolution can further offer us, which was previously impossible. UN-
Studio uses the example of the line to summarize architecture in
a graphic and ideogrammatic way. The extremes of this line used
to be well defined prior to the arrival of digital technology as a
balancing of an aesthetic on the one end and functionality on the
other. This was the fundamental paradigm within which the "traditional" architect designed. The architectural profession was well
defined and with clear limits. Its boundaries were of art on the
one hand and engineering on the other. What has changed over
the past twenty years with the digitization of society and thus that
of architecture? Today's architect has the opportunity to extend
this line, to interact with new skills and new fields that have been
integrated into the definition of architecture, such as digital art,
43 fashion and virtual reality. At the same time, the concept of functionality has turned towards efficiency, where efficiency is cou-
pled with abstract values; such as the catalytic power of a building, its economy, energy performance, and all the broader parameters within which the building meets a contemporary context.
The image itself influences the efficiency of an architectural project. The skill level of communication and of visual expression has
a decisive impact. The envelope, as previously mentioned, is the
bearer of abstract values fundamental to integrating a building
within an urban and societal context. This feature becomes the
fundamental vehicle of dialogue between client and architect. So,
while debating the meaning of digital thinking in architecture,
UNStudio places much emphasis on expanding the limits of the
line. They argue that the original perception of the line is limiting
and a circle better represents their new vision. A circle, internal to
the design process, obscures the limits of where an aesthetic and a
function begin and end. The loop of the circle allows for complex
connections and interactions that cross-reference each other.
They work within this hybrid and fluid platform that adapts itself
continuously to changing circumstances and different local and
global sites.

"We are expanding the possibilities of architecture. We should start by pla-
cing these potentials in a circle. It is a quite interesting way of not defining

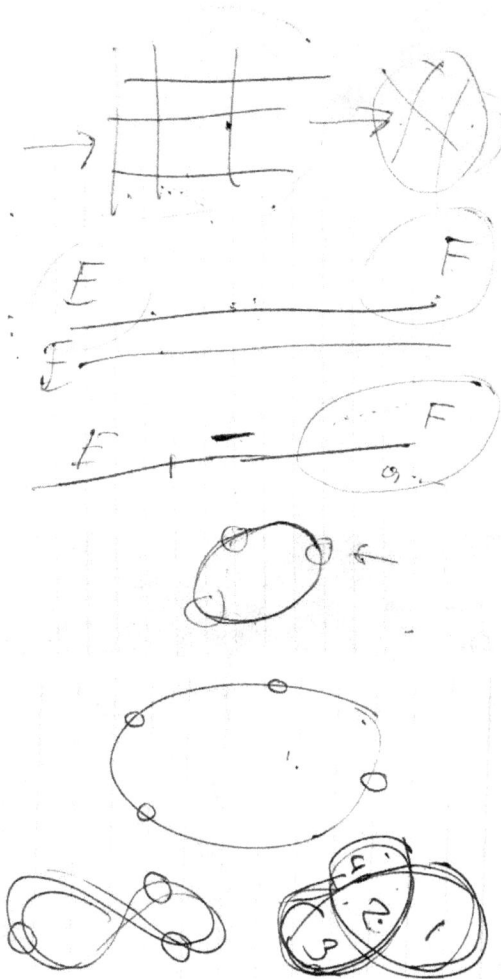

B. Van Berkel,
Sketches

*The transition from the modernist grid (equals potential) to a continuous but expanded fluid system (multiple potentials). In the modernist model, repetition did not provide for mutations. The structure was rigid. "We expand the possibilities of architecture, like aligning them on a circle and not trying to clearly delineate where the aesthetic or functionality begin and end" (Van Berkel09).*

*Digital technology offers the opportunity to work with more fluid and complex structures in which the repetition is not modular, but adaptable. "E" and "F" represent aesthetic and function. These two points were previously rigid and clearly identified the limits of architecture. In the contemporary model proposed by Van Berkel, they mix and mingle on a continuous line, endless and constantly evolving up to the diagram for the Mercedes Benz Museum in Stuttgart (see bottom sketch).*

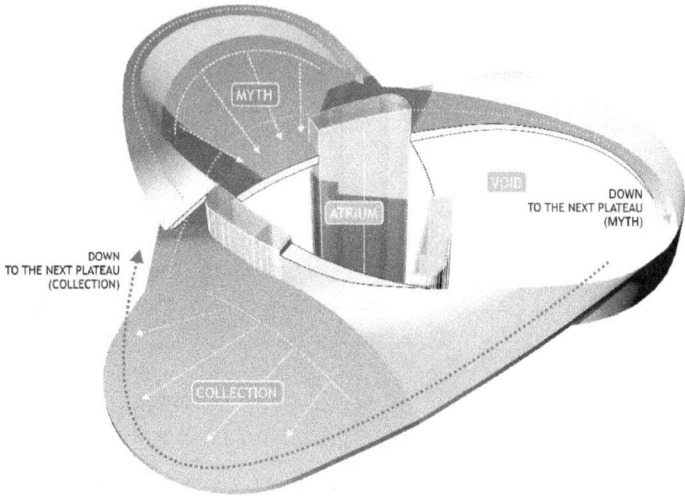

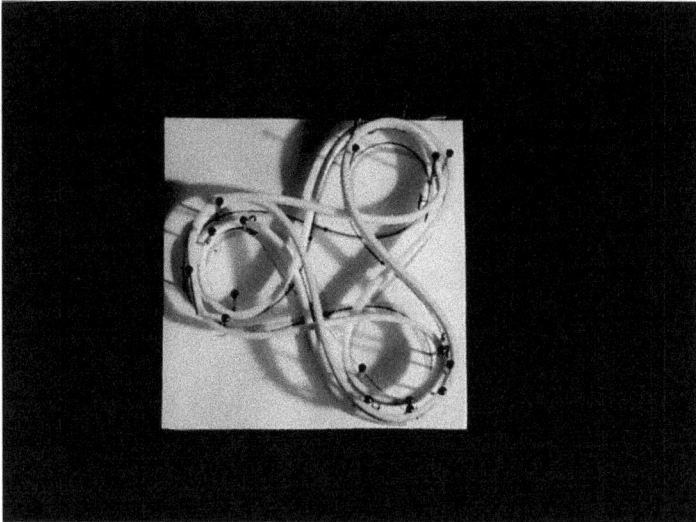

MERCEDES BENZ MUSEUM, STUTTGART, GERMANY, 2001-2006

*The program of use and the geometry develop along a continuous loop, creating a repeatable model that is theoretically infinite. This same scheme establishes the path of travel inside the museum.*

where aesthetic or functionality can be found exactly. So today you cannot so quickly define where one ends and where the other begins." (Van Berkel 09)

In the modernist model, the instrument of the grid was based on the repetition of a modular. The modular did not provide for mutations; the structure remained rigid and rational. Digital technology has introduced the ability to work with more fluid and complex forms where the repetition is not sequential, but adaptable. The organizing principle is what is repeated and the resultant design process is less linear and rational. Digital design develops via iterations and optimizations. UNStudio is chiefly concerned with the enormous possibilities that these new structures are fluid and open to tapping the hidden potential of complex systems. The studio often employs the word "to unfold"; signifying an opening up and unwrapping. They emphasize that what appears at the end of their process is unknown to them at the beginning, and through complex processes one may reveal an unknown potential in a design that offers an unforeseen architecture. Their design model for the Mercedes-Benz Museum in Stuttgart is a good example of [44] an architecture generated through a circular and cyclical methodology of continuity within which differing formal, functional, and programmatic aspects interact and are not individually identifiable. They create a continuous space through which visitors can travel as a passenger in a car, and combine this with a mixed-use program requiring different display needs. The space functions alternate along a single continuous loop while referencing a centrally organizing geometry, where different needs interact and intervene on each other transforming the final formal result. It is impossible to identify and isolate a particular solution which satisfies a requirement, it is always a "give-and-take" (as defined by Van Berkel) between the program, building techniques and the formal requirements.

Aesthetics and functionality are combined into a single creative design effort. This project manifests their search for organizational principles that can be simultaneously consistent while formally flexible. Their conceptual framework offers adaptable boundaries without compromising the integrity of a continuously flowing space that is non-repetitive and transformative. In this case UNStudio's digital thinking is concretized in an open complex program traveling along a continuous line and not through the traditional design approach of accumulation and aggregation of independent closed spaces. The introduction of a single guiding system that offers variable capacities to a project will generate new and unexpected worlds and fields of research. Their use of creative models for an intelligent design, indefinitely renewable, is an invention that concisely synthesizes UNStudio's "digital thinking".

## 2.6 Project development: sustainable digital design

The applicable potentials of this process are numerous and revealing. The creation and management of a digital model is effective only if it provides the organizing principle and framework from the very beginning of the project. This provides the platform for adapting and transforming the entire design in a relatively short time to changing production, technical or formal needs. Toward this purpose UNStudio created, for the Mercedes-Benz Museum, a hierarchical digital model that allowed for the constant updating of the project and facilitated the information exchange between the many team professionals involved in the construction phase of the project. A specialized team within UNStudio dealt exclusively with the management of this huge digital material; linking all the various entities involved in the project. This is an absolute necessity for containing both budget and schedule in works of this complexity. Van Berkel and Bos assert that with the right management and organization of digital frameworks of the project, one can create complex and innovative works with a cost increase of only 3%, and that this is only possible if the project is built and designed, since its genesis, within a design model that responds rigorously to established formal and geometric rules. The architect is not only responsible for creating the formal moves. The management methodology is as important as the aesthetic scope and today's intelligence and creative potential of digital technology require a new mindset with new frameworks. UNStudio took the opportunity of designing the Mercedes Benz Museum in Stuttgart to create an internal studio team of specialists dedicated to the management of the project's digital material. This group of specialists took charge of managing the digital structure of the project in its various aspects from conceptual design through construction management. The resulting three-dimensional model

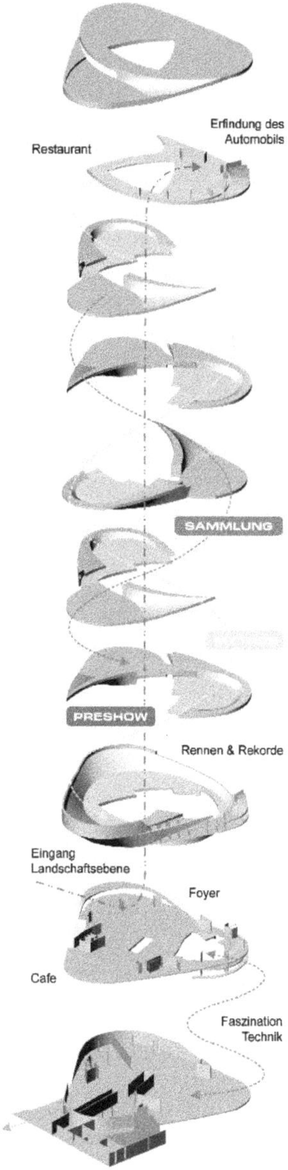

Erfindung des
Automobils

Restaurant

SAMMLUNG

PRESHOW

Rennen & Rekorde

Eingang
Landschaftsebene

Foyer

Cafe

Faszination
Technik

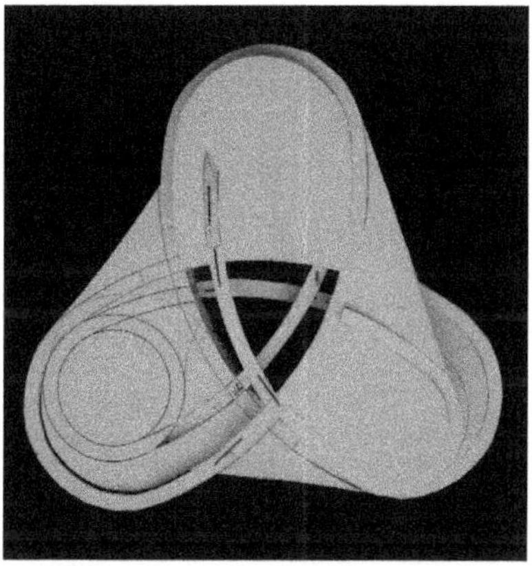

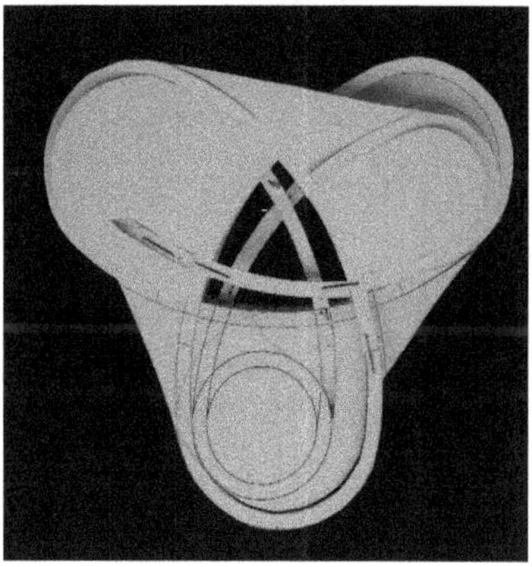

MERCEDES BENZ MUSEUM, STUTTGART,
GERMANY, 2001-2006

*Distribution diagram and photos of study
models. Two elevators travel to the top floor
where the visitor can choose two different paths
along which to descend through the whole
museum. The two courses (collection tour and
legend tour) intersect each floor, allowing
visitors to choose a new direction.*

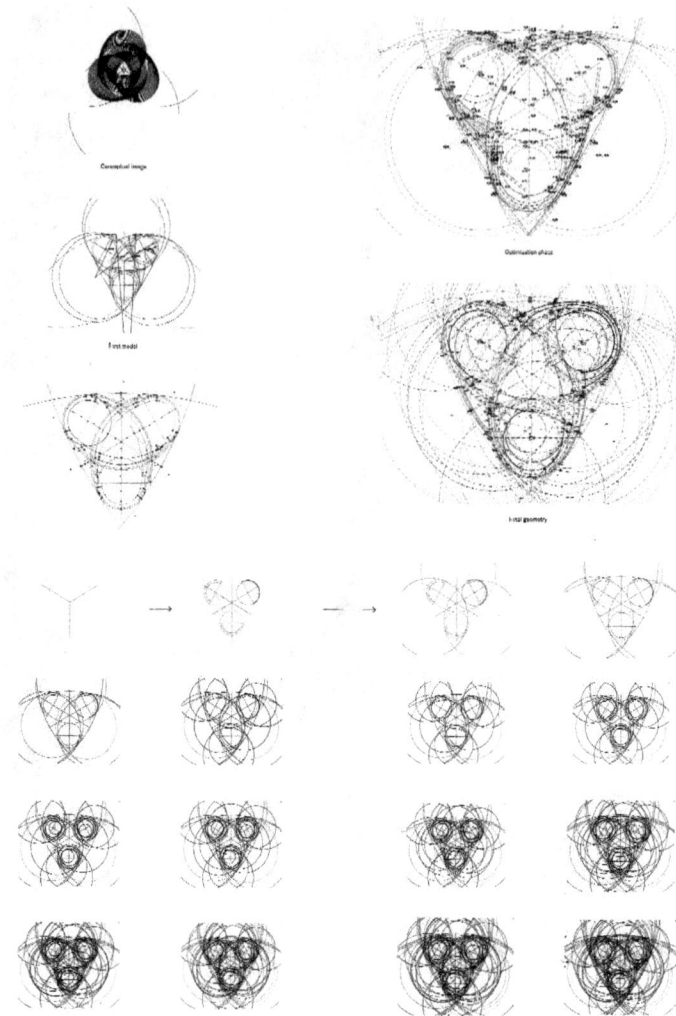

MERCEDES BENZ MUSEUM, STUTTGART, GERMANY, 2001-2006

*Parametric geometric studies: The building form and plans are the result of precise geometric constructions. In a parametric model three-dimensional geometries are the direct expression of mathematical formulas. This allows the designers to manage the project shape with a hierarchical model that can make changes relatively quickly.*

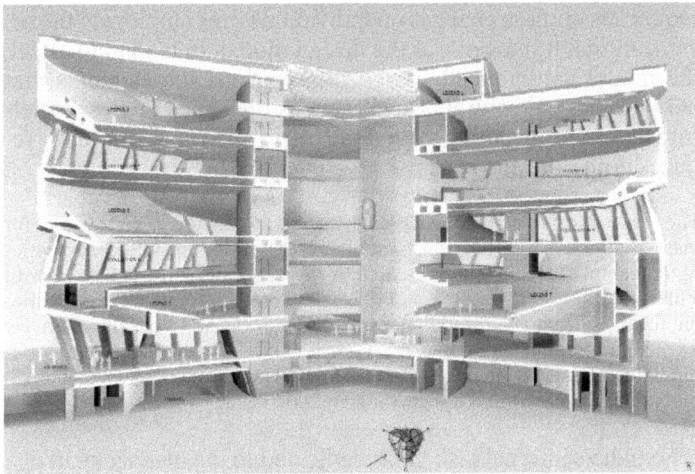

MERCEDES BENZ MUSEUM, STUTTGART, GERMANY, 2001-2006

*Computer generated three-dimensional models. The three-dimensional computer modeling is not limited to simply defining geometric shapes that are aesthetically pleasing. It can be used to manage specific data and technical information, which maximizes the constructability and budget efficiency of the project.*

was so complex, organized in hierarchical parameters; it required the help of specialized technicians as dedicated full-time staff. This digital team, if well thought out, can be an incredible aid to designers who cannot expend their energies and abilities on computer programming and modeling at this level of complexity. The task should be delegated to specialists who work daily to upgrade digital model and at the same time are in constant contact with the team of designers. The museum was designed so that the changing parts or details could be applied and verified in a "rippling" format throughout the entire project. For example, the

51,52 structure of the reinforced concrete walls that defined the spiral of the exhibition space could be altered during the planning phase in accordance with the technical and structural requirements of the engineers. The modified curvature and shape of the septa was then incorporated into the model that assessed through its digital hierarchy any consequences affecting the form and space. In a traditional process, this would involve the laborious reshaping and redesigning the entire design in all its parts.

In contrast, an intelligent digital model can quickly test the consequences of these changes on individual items employing the organizational framework of the design model. In a domino effect, the model automatically renews the various sub-elements that

52 define the architectural design, such as the shape of glass panels rather than re-inventing the overall infrastructure. This greatly reduces both time and cost.

The hierarchical structure creates a "living model", an inconceivable tool for many traditional activities, which simultaneously opens up multiple activities fundamental to architectural research. A project represented in CAAD with a hierarchical system becomes not only completely different from a traditional form ,(since it is a three-dimensional rendering, and basically relatively negligible component) , to become a precise "model" that allows one to manipulate a changing and open structure toward the simulation of a real possibility one can pursue and design. (Saggio, 2007, p. 88)

UNStudio's internal task force, dedicated to the management of a project's digital model, acts as a fundamental meeting point between the UNStudio designers and the various elements external to the studio. The digital team becomes the focal point through which all information and disciplines pass. It provides common ground for discussion and exchange between the different parties

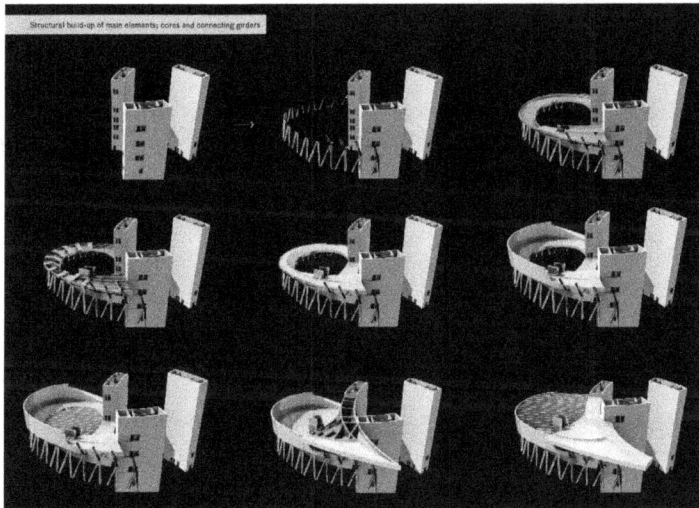

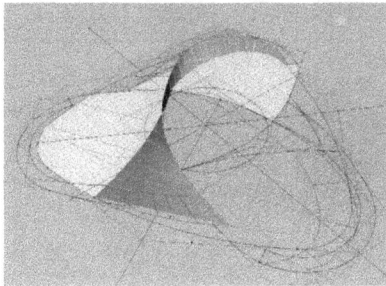

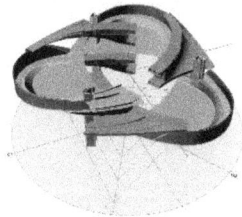

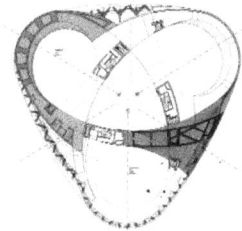

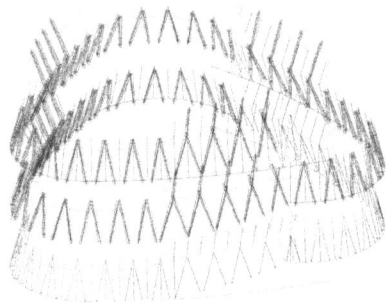

MERCEDES BENZ MUSEUM, STUTTGART, GERMANY, 2001-2006

*Above: the structural components, the three load-bearing bodies central to the building. Below: the facade perimeter support system. At the center: digital model of the Twist.*

MERCEDES BENZ MUSEUM,
STUTTGART, GERMANY, 2001-2006

*Above: drawings for concrete
formwork. Mathematical modeling
controls allowed quick calculations
of the required geometric
specifications for the formwork.
Below: 1:1 scale model of the Twist
built on-site.*

MERCEDES BENZ MUSEUM, STUTTGART, GERMANY, 2001-2006

*Three-dimensional detail of the façade.*

and as such requires a highly skilled and dedicated staff.

For the design and construction of this project, a three-dimensio-
49  nal model (mother model) was created that based itself on rein-
terpreting the initial two-dimensional design for the competition.
In the mother model, generated by Arnold Walt in Germany together with UNStudio, the building was split into more than one
hundred mathematical parameters that organized and defined
the geometry. This made it possible to develop and adapt the design efficiently and rapidly under a compressed schedule of time.
One of the many design problems this approach helped manage
and resolve into the project's formal aspects, were the demands of
multiple technical elements. These were input and run through
the digital mother model which coordinated such as items as: the
irregularly shaped 6,500 glass panels for the facade, the penetra-
tions in the concrete surface (of double curvature) for lighting
and fire detection devices and the collocation and sizing of metal
panels on the exterior.

"Without this rigorous management of the geometry there would not have
been such freedom in the architecture. Managing the mother model reduces
the risks of mistakes and miscalculations; it helps to achieve an economy of
materials, and makes the building process controllable. It is called digital sustainability." (Van Berkel 06)

51  The building is structurally organized around three load-bearing
concrete central bodies that incorporate stairs and vertical connections. The rest of the structure is defined by a series of brid-
ging elements with span over 30 meters that define the various
52  exhibition spaces. These parts are connected by a concrete structure, called a "twist" that creates a frame of beams that transfer
the floors loads to the facade and central core. In addition to beams supporting the large floor slabs of the exhibition areas, the
structure is supported by rhythmic colonnade of variable section
encircling the geometry of the building.
52  The "twist" element required a customized analysis: There were
four points in the building geometry where the ceiling of the exhibition space, called the "legend room", became a vertical wall
connecting directly to the exhibition spaces between them. Since
this condition encompassed two floors, it served as a shell structure within which equipment rooms and services were embedded.
During the construction phase, a 1:1 scale model was built of the

complex structure which would not have been possible without the modeling and calculation aid of computer programs. It should also be stated that all technical systems, lighting, ventilation, safety and environmental management were incorporated within the concrete structure itself. This increased the difficulties in the design stage, but made the whole project more coherent and comprehensive; increasing its abstract and evocative quality. This type of design process increases the organization and design articulation period prior to construction:

> "The competition phase was followed by a six-month pre-planning phase, in order to minimize risks, (regarding costs, timing and design concept), investigate financing variants, and to meet the prescribed budgets before the green light for planning and realization could be given and the design approved." (Van Berkel 06)

## 2.7 The programmatic dimension

Society has change as well as the manner of living in a city. A search for new forms is the natural result of these changes. The rhythms and routines of work, life, and entertainment in the contemporary age follow new dynamics with new transportation means, communication methods and relationships. How can one create urban spaces with tools capable to evaluate these new conditions? UNStudio responds through research and testing of organizational principles and generators that lie beneath the surface. Van Berkel and Bos identify and study the nervous system and musculature of the contemporary world as the heart of their research. One can arrive at a truly innovative architecture by applying these principles in depth. Digital tools and an approach of responsive digital thinking can grasp and fully develop the potential that this new field puts at our disposal.

As mentioned above, the ability to abstract is an essential first step for the designer. The city or the house will no longer be perceived as a mere accumulation of squares, walls, buildings, facades [13] and roads but, it will become a complex layered body, with ever changing flows and forces, where chaos, business value, or man himself, to name a few, are potential assets that can be abstracted and captured within complex analytical models.

The digital material is fluid and adaptable. The generative and geometric principle is hidden in the organism's memory; encryp-

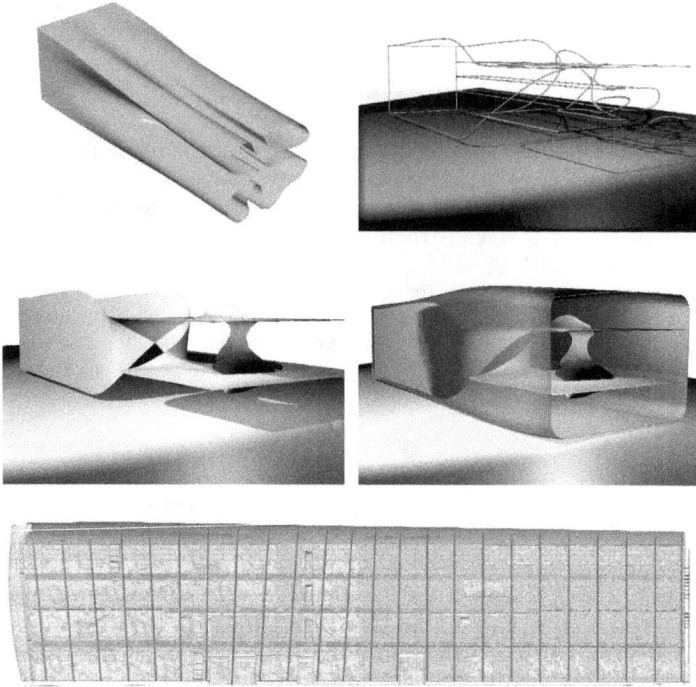

GRAZ THEATRE,
GRAZ, AUSTRIA,
2008,
BLOB-TO-BOX

*Diagrams and photos of the exterior facade. The blob-to-box model traces the transition from public spaces, the highly expressive entrance foyer, to the more technical and restricted spaces of stage and backstage.*

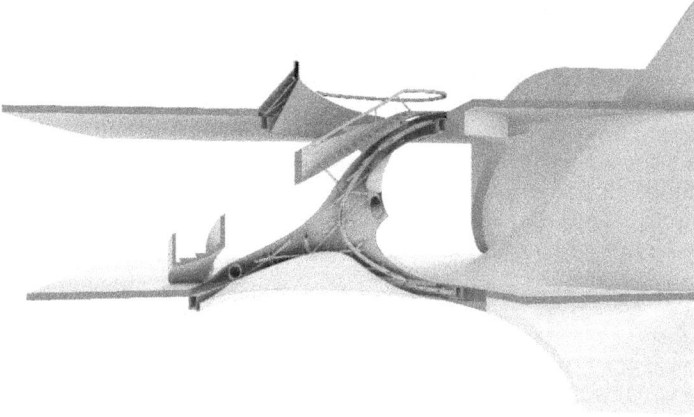

GRAZ THEATRE, GRAZ, AUSTRIA, 2008
*Photograph and perspectival section of the spiral staircase in the theatre foyer.*

ted with strict and complex codes and relationships involving, by
their very nature, change and transformation. The concept of
56 "Blob to Box" is important precisely for this reason: the process
smoothly and completely transforms the formal result, but without ever changing the relationships and internal connections of
the system. Furthermore, what makes it even more interesting
and innovative is the possibility of bringing to life and creating
spaces somewhere between the initial configuration and the final
outcome. The fields of connection and hybridization are the new
areas of the digital. With this in mind, UNStudio experiments
with new organizational systems, programs and space placement
along trajectories capable of expanding the project's potential.
Van Berkel and Bos act as middle men, "between art and air-
ports", between engineering and architecture. They reject ideological positions and search within the interstitial spaces of society
and culture; those places where frictions are strongest and offer a
stimulus to research and design. The subjects of infrastructural
nodes and industrial buildings become a research field specific to
UNStudio. The overlapping and commingling of different class
levels of society are reflected in the overlapping multiple components of the architecture. A concept of "inclusiveness", as termed
by Van Berkel and Bos, is key to understanding the UNStudio design spirit.

"Blob or box – it doesn't matter anymore. To redefine organizational structures in an inclusive way means to proportion all information at the basis of
the project in one, comprehensive system" (Van Berkel, Bos 08, pag. 223)

Today's architect is required more than ever to have a well-roun-
ded knowledge of multiple areas and no longer works with di-
sconnected components. A contemporary design rationale is based on a global gesture aimed at absorbing all differences. Likewise, the digital approach is global: Such concepts and such ways
of thinking and understanding design is born directly of digital
media, the computer, internet databases; with their various virtual
display options that make possible the materialization of these
complex worlds and systems in real time.
The different possible computer techniques: wireframe, rendering, technical drafting, become simple and interactive tools for
the designer; who can develop them either independently or su-
perimposed to create synthesized images that make possible the

full coordination of different project components. This simultaneous visualization often reveals that conflicting parts and structures of the project, that may highlight problems and critical junctures, may just as well open up new and unforeseen creative dimensions. All this happens in a completely three-dimensional environment, in which the object architecture is no longer the fruit of plans and perspective, but is created as a spatial object and a generator of spaces. New calculation and design tools enable these digital theories to be materialized in the real world. The ability to parameterize abstract values and link them to shapes, sizes and volumes creates a new design method that greatly simplifies the ability to verify and test these complex organisms. The design of the organizational model and of the relationships and connections between spaces and different disciplines requires a large investment in terms of time and effort by the designers. If the organizational model is well developed and structured, the rest of the project will proceed in a smooth and efficient manner. Formal options can be tested quickly without affecting the fundamental organizing principle that anchors the design research.

In pursuit of this design research, UNStudio often works on infrastructure or industrial programs or with large and complex mixed-use systems. They focus on finding new ways to organize and give shape to the city. Tools such as *Deep Planning* and *Mobil Forces* have proven to be essential in giving shape and coherence to their research. Many of these studies, especially at the urban level, have yet to be built. The design for the Ponte Parodi in Genoa [61, 62, 64] will be a very interesting test-case for evaluating the urban response to a city-wide design that is guided by the principles and formal organization of coexistence for different activities during a twenty-four hour period. The three-dimensional shape and organization of this square are the result of patterns analyses and possible dynamics between different programs in relation to the day.

## 2.8 Ponte Parodi, continuous and endless organization

In 2001, UNStudio won the international competition for the redevelopment of the port of Genoa. The competition formed part of a wider project to upgrade and redevelop the city of Genoa and the outdated port no longer met the city's needs. The area under consideration, the Ponte Parodi, was a large quay in the center of the port formerly occupied by an industrial zone. The site was dominated by a large grain silo in a very strategic area that connected to the historic center. Situated in the middle of the port, between the ferry terminal and the area of the Old Port, was the town's tourist area which hosts architectural interventions made by Renzo Piano for the Columbus celebrations of 1992.

61 The UNStudio design and program of use are complexly articulated both in programmatic and formal terms. Their new square on the Mediterranean, as it is called, contains three thematic zones to be occupied over a twenty-four hour period: The "Music and Knowledge" zone provides an auditorium, a nightclub and other interactive forums with virtual reality exhibitions. The "Leisure and Sport" zone offers squash courts, a climbing gym, a swimming pool, a fitness center and athletic fields. The third zone of "Journeys and Discoveries" provides for new cruise terminal with dedicated boating facilities. All three programmatic zones integrate the required infrastructure; each with its own commercial and public services (travel agencies, banks, rental agencies, post offices, agencies, etc.). The project will create circa 450 new jobs and employ an average of 600 people during its construction phase.

The design program is as complex in formal and functional terms as it is in its phasing. The city seeks to continually expand its historic center towards the sea and thereby sew up an old scar that
61 severs the city from both port and waterfront. Like all urban projects of this scale, one must likewise absorb the different forces and pressures that gravitate towards it. Politics, the city, inflation and construction techniques are factors that weigh heavily on the final design and should be actively incorporated in the creative process. The firm's past experience developing multiple models that guide and give coherence to a design is fundamental to the commission.

Such a project would not have existed without the accumulated knowledge and techniques from UNStudio's principles of *Deep-Planning, Inclusive Principle* and, in the specific case of the Ponte Parodi, the *V-model*. These three principles are not applied in a literal manner but act a reservoir of knowledge and techniques to be interpreted internally by the studio. The design for the Ponte Parodi is the manifestation of UNStudio's cumulative research of the effects of fluid and evolving information, data and processes on the architectural field.

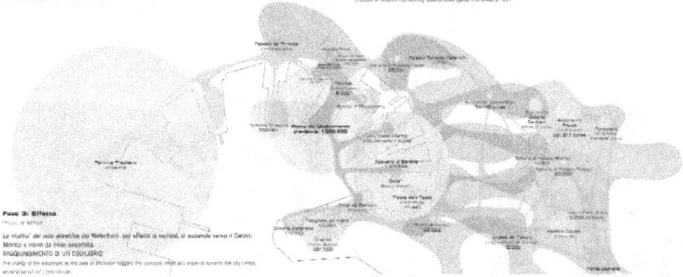

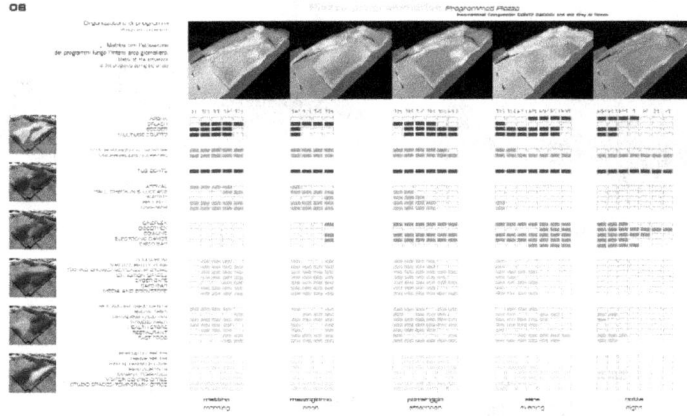

PONTE PARODI, GENOA, ITALY, 2001-2011

*Diagrams of urban analysis measuring daily and weekly activity levels. "Thanks to diagrammatic tools and digital technology, UNStudio was able to maximize the potential of the project and on this basis, determine the best course for adapting it to the formal aspect of architecture."*

*Above: Time-tracking diagrams analyzing the different activity levels in the plaza.*

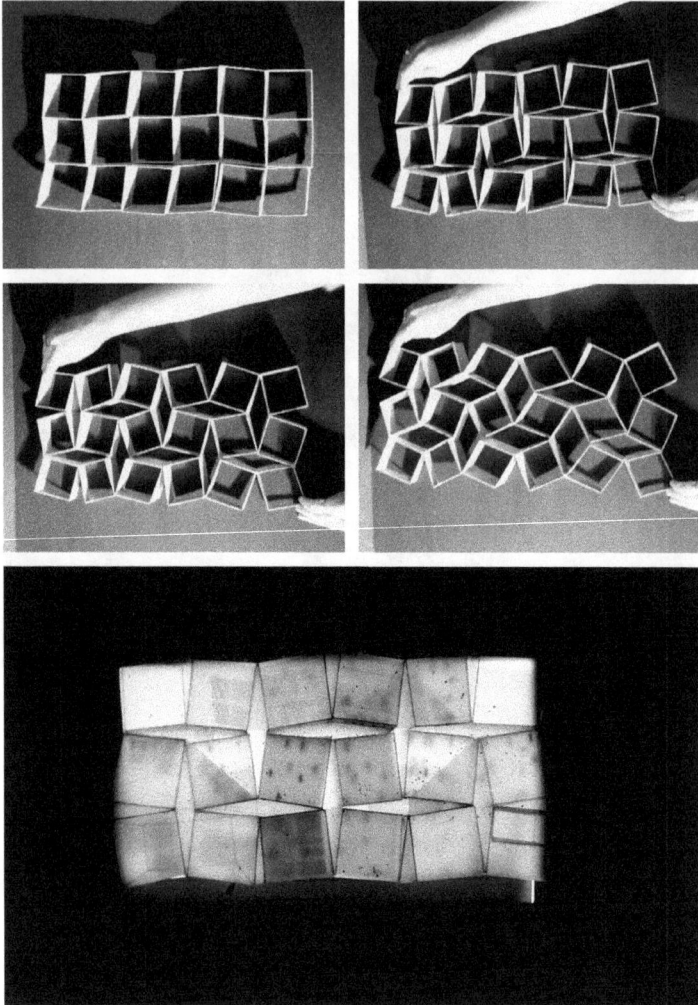

PONTE PARODI, GENOA, ITALY, 2001-2011

*"The grid is deformed and selectively opened up in its orthogonal structure. It provides an ideal format for the management of technical and functional spaces such as parking in the basement, and creates interstitial spaces that allow diamond-shaped vertical connections, day lighting the lower floors. It provides a structural net and maximizes flexibility for spatial and formal configurations."*

UNStudio's Ponte Parodi is a clear and concise proposal. The new square on the Mediterranean is both a three-dimensional plaza and a mechanism for creative activities and movement over a daily twenty-four hour span. This need resulted from research and analysis of the city. Their analysis of urban space was not reduced to a traditional two-dimensional floor plan, which may over simplify and gloss-over contradictory and problematic elements. Rather, UNStudio expanded their analysis to include topological conditions, the forces, and principles that affected quality of life in Genoa. These factors were integrated with a time factor and summarized into diagrams and parameters of analysis aimed at systematizing the city model. The goal was to generate a space that was not a superficial interpretation of Genoa but to replicate and multiply the qualities and experiences inherent to the city into an architectural, three-dimensional and contemporary space. The complexity and presence of different programs, patterns, landscapes, flows, was not simplified but was enhanced; individual components were not isolated and flattened but made to interact. The Ponte Parodi design strives to recreate the qualities of the contemporary city, enhanced by Rem Koolhaas' "Delirious New York", via an urban mechanism that does not flatten itself into a closed system. This strategy creates new possibilities for organizing space into fluid and complex systems that allow for an open-ended narrative. Modernity lies in this new methodology of cumulative and generative programs in a constant exchange between architectural space, intended use and the landscape. Thanks to diagrammatic tools and digital technology, UNStudio was able to maximize the potential of the project and on this basis, determine the best course for adapting it to the formal aspect of architecture.

"This diagram of the 360 degree circle of experience, representing the per- 63 spective of a future visitor, conveys the potential of site-specific, topological conditions together with time-and use-related variables. As the project emerges by relating these values to each other in order to find the optimal combination, it is clear that the focus of the design throughout has been to create the ultimate user experience" (Van Berkel, Bos 06 page. 292)

Their process is always one of wave-like optimization and reaches a final configuration only after multiple iterations have been manipulated by complex project specific influences and factors.

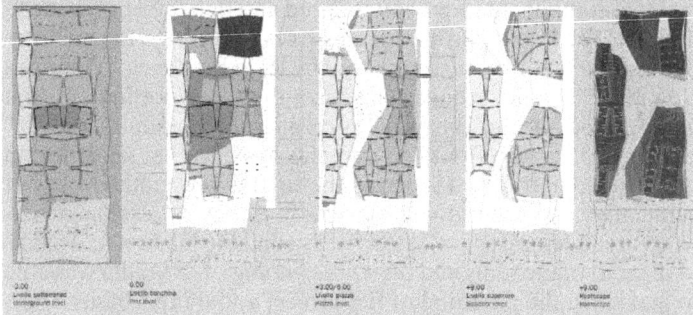

PONTE PARODI, GENOA, ITALY, 2001-2011

*Above: rendering of Ponte Parodi's Mediterranean plaza.*
*Center: plans of 3 of the 5 plaza levels.*
*Below: View of the waterfront.*

At this point let us identify the formal system, the geometric model of reference that turns these ambitions into an intelligent and coherent building to be constructed. The geometric model is especially important in projects this large and complex. The Mercedes Benz Museum is a relevant example of a project built with a geometric system. It is intelligently organized and a structured methodology is the only way to achieve similar projects of efficiency that avoid unnecessary costs, materials, time and energy.

There are four basic conditions at Ponte Parodi to which the geometric system must respond: flexible use in a complex program, structural requirements, landscaping requirements and the need, through the three-dimensional plaza, to bring natural daylight to the lower levels.

UNStudio intuitively creates spaces and organizes the project wi-  62
thin a deformed grid. The grid is an established design tool often criticized by Van Berkel and Bos, as the bearer of "equal potential". In this case however, a flexible and fluid grid is what is required. The grid is deformed and selectively opened up in its or-  62
thogonal structure. It provides an ideal format for the management of technical and functional spaces such as parking in the lower levels, and creates interstitial spaces that allow diamond-shaped vertical connections that day light the lower floors. The fluid grid provides a structural net and maximizes flexibility for spatial and formal configurations.

The grid acts three-dimensionally and its diamond-shaped section exploits the same "V" model conceptual prototype of the Arnhem train station. This "V" model originates at the Erasmus Bridge in Rotterdam and develops into the Ponte Parodi where it is equally suited to the program needs and manifests itself as a multi-directional, three-dimensional structure of itself

The concept allows for a complex, continuity and fluidity of space that in single gesture integrates the various levels of the plaza with the many technical and organizational requirements of the project.

How does the digital enter the project? What has digital thought brought that would otherwise not have been possible?

There are several things to consider and analyze. Let us start from  62, 64
a technical and practical standpoint: the definition of a three-dimensional grid. The digital model began by defining the grid in response to specific technical and structural requirements. Once

the formal idea was defined, it became possible to create a digital model that took into account the various parameters such as minimum and maximum frame lights, angles for light penetration and programmatic needs. This model, around which the project took shape, could be changed and updated and monitored in real time according to different needs and simultaneously communicate the formal impact. At the same time, one could manipulate in reverse by intervening with formal moves without affecting the basic structure of the project. These formal changes would occur within a range of variables determined by the technical requirements and architectural decisions. This approach, in addition to providing consistency and discipline from a creative point of view to the project, also increased efficiency of project development and management.

Diagrammatic and analytical tools were also overlaid on the model in order to define and identify different uses within the program, The hub of the operation was the recreation of a piece of city that over twenty-four hours made the most of the potential offered by the site and the project. To define this hub, the use of diagrams integrated with the time function was a very effective tool that allowed, in a concise and interactive way, the insertion all its many aspects. The findings and decisions resulting from this analysis were then applied to the three-dimensional mesh of the project thus defining the project parameters.

My last point may seem trivial, but it is essential to underline: what changed here was the designers' initial and overall approach to the project. The architectural design is no longer regarded as a mere creation of forms and functions satisfying a need, or the quest for an absolute masterpiece, but it is the materialization of a set of concepts, data and information contained within a system-mechanism design, generating opportunities for both the architect in terms of design and for future building users and managers. In a well-planned system, there corresponds an architectural mechanism that is both convincing and functional where within the functionality, as described above, a variety of concepts and values apply that go far beyond the sphere of traditional practice and technology. Behind the design there exists a sea of information and knowledge, logic and organizational structures that represent the true essence of the project.

The design is a demonstration, not the only possible one, of a way of thinking and understanding of architectural space. Ponte Parodi, as well as the Merced Benz Museum, IFCCA in New York or the Arnhem Central Station, along with many other projects can be considered as one larger macro-project that revolves around the same themes, or as the various manifestations and applications of a like-minded design. The space before becoming physical is a mental space. The construction and design of a methodology that employs the digital as a tool and engine for interpretation and creation of architectural space, represents to UNStudio the invaluable asset of the IT revolution to contemporary architecture.

# 3. Form, fluidity and soft interactivity

Van Berkel and Bos' research of flexible, interactive, time-sensitive and dynamic mental constructs and organizational frameworks manifests in a variety of formal languages within the UNStudio designs.

Their aesthetic language is made up of continuous planes, fluid volumes and geometries that respond to a creative process that is user-based. They immerse the user into an architectural space of innovative formal structures. Traditional Euclidean geometry is surpassed by the studio's research in the digital design process and by their application of new building materials and technologies through invention and experimentation. Engineering and technical components become one with the new architectural systems they generate. For UNStudio, technological and scientific advances become opportunities to expand the field of architecture, to stretch its limits, and to understand its new parameters and responses. Contemporary Dutch architecture has always been in the forefront of a movement towards a balance of technology and art; between service and cultural stimulus. It has often succeeded in this difficult task by not only incorporating these two extremes but by actively engages them with one another. This architecture generates a complicity in which art and technology are actively collaborating and expands their definitions well beyond ideological limits.

[69] The forms and expression of UNStudio's designs are generated from within, coming as natural and necessary solutions to a creative process which, although not beginning as a sculptural form, does not deny the power and importance of the aesthetic as a fundamental communicator of content in architecture. It would be contradictory, if not impossible, to package UNStudio's programmatic, methodological and abstract research within traditional volumes and materials. The attempt would be equivalent to playing electronic music on a harpsichord, or coercing a synthesizer to perform Bach.

New technologies and inventions enrich our world of perception and of knowledge. The formal language of UNStudio's research is one of continuity and fluidity. It contrasts against the traditional modernist grid; where repetition, standardization, and the reduction of architectural forms and systems into reproducible series

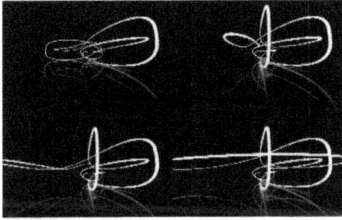

THE CHANGING ROOM, VENICE, ITALY, 2008

*The pavilion design investigates the relationship between material, space and man. Inspired by trends in the fashion world, it dematerializes a classical architectural vocabulary by employing tools and requirements that are foreign to the field. Above: Conceptual diagrams. Below: Construction photographs of the pavilion in the architectural exhibition space of the Venice Biennial.*

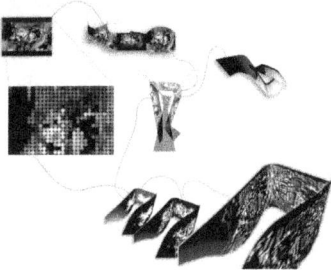

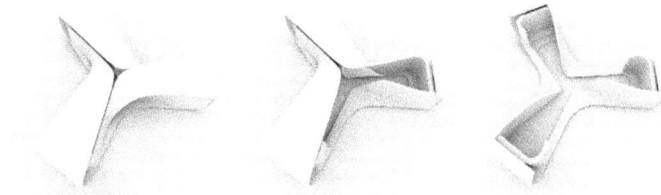

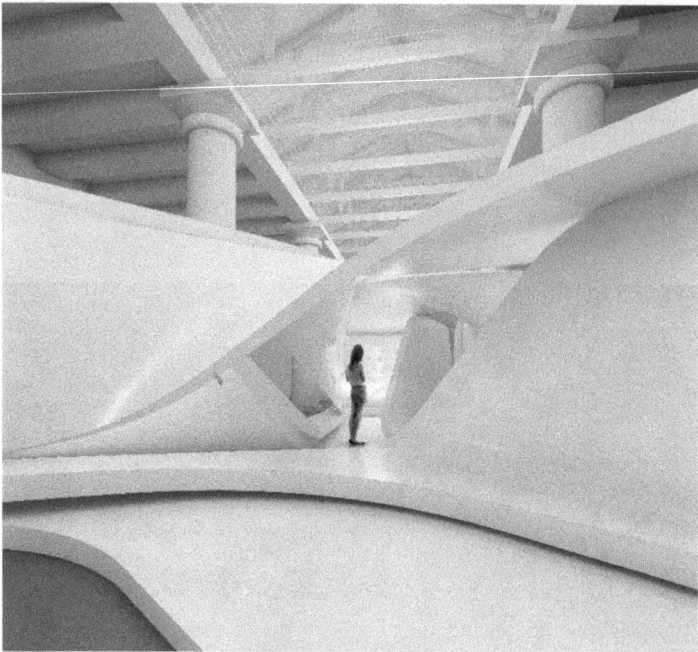

THE CHANGING ROOM, VENICE, ITALY, 2008
*Photograph and rendering of the pavilion.*

THE CHANGING ROOM,
VENICE, ITALY, 2008

*Photograph of the pavilion interior.*

with often aggregated results led to an impersonal, alienating architecture that is no longer viable. Today, personalization, adaptability, interaction and transformation are paramount requirements and technological developments have made it possible to respond, even in complex architectural systems, to these demands.

## 3.1 Installations and small worlds

UNStudio uses small scale projects such as temporary installations, pavilions and exhibition spaces to test formal systems, concepts and technologies. A small scale allows for more radical experimentation with quick results that increase the designers' knowledge and techniques to be applied later on future larger scaled projects. Their design research on the formal aspects of an endless surface is made evident in The Changing Room at the 2008 Venice Biennale, in the 2009 Burnham Pavilion in Chicago and in the Pavilion for the Milan Triennial of 1996. Walls and floor merge into a single surface. Openings are neither windows nor doorways, but reduced to fissures along the different planes that envelop, open-up, and slide past each other. Visual trajectories are continuous and the eye glides along these running surfaces without points of discontinuity. The volume envelops and immerses the viewer in a dynamic new dimension where thresholds between different chambers and functions of the pavilions are imperceptible. A conceptual flow is rendered literal here and provides for a global sensory experience by the user.

At the same time the themes and programs of these micro cosmos investigate areas related to the de-materialization of space, the definition of new types of formal communication with the digital virtual reality and interactivity. Perceptual experiences are often the main force that generates these pavilions. Technological research is driven to extremes and scientific innovation is exploited to its full potential for new forms that address the relationship between man and the space he inhabits.

Many projects also respond to specific functional requirements. The "Theatre of Immanence" or the 2009 New Amsterdam Plein & Pavilion in New York combine form with function. The smaller scale of these projects provides for a more immediate testing of a digital methodology. This methodology seeks to arrive at a form that embodies a wave-like design process of optimization between

69, 70, 71
73, 74, 75, 76

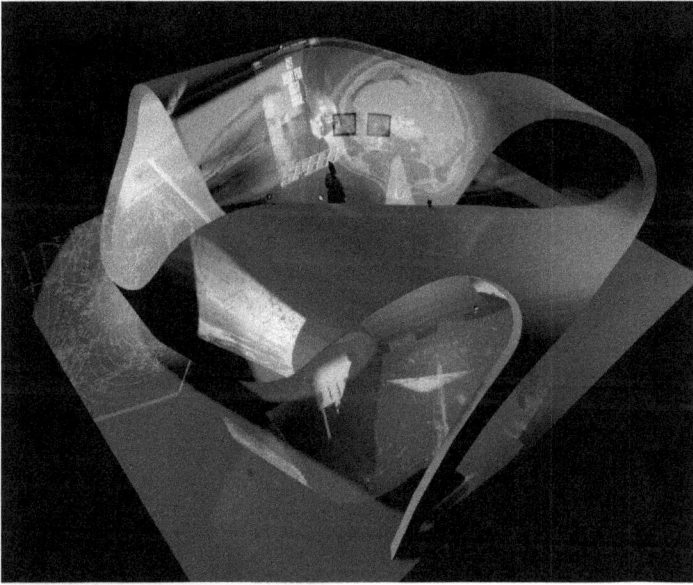

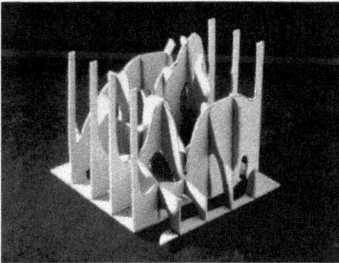

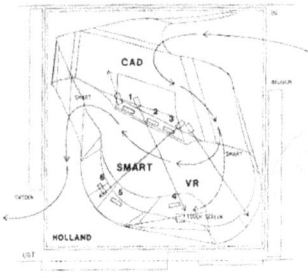

PAVILION FOR THE MILAN TRIENNIAL,
MILAN, ITALY, 1996

*"The small scale allows for more radical
experimentation with quick results that
increase their knowledge and techniques
to be applied later on future larger
scaled projects."*

ANDREA SOLLAZZO

BURNHAM PAVILLION, NEW YORK, USA, 2009

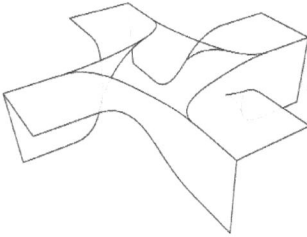

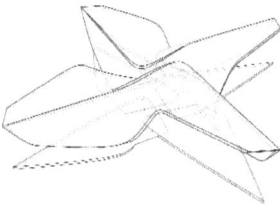

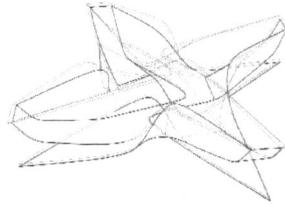

NEW AMSTERDAM PLEIN PAVILION, NEW YORK, USA, 2008-2009

*"The computerized ability to create three-dimensional molds or patterns for the cutting of the individual components makes it possible to execute these forms relatively quickly and with enormous precision."*

NEW AMSTERDAM PLEIN PAVILION, NEW YORK, USA, 2008-2009

THE THEATRE OF IMMANENCE, FRANKFURT ON THE RHINE, GERMANY, 2007
*View of the digital model.*

practical needs and geometric systems. The "Theatre of Immanence" was part of an exhibition that involved many artists and architects, whose theme was the space of communication.

"A common thread to all the projects is that they address the social and inter     76, 78
relational aspects of communication or spaces of communication. In this manner the projects insist on the relevance of art and architecture to which new technology can only add but not change the basic missions or functions. Needless to say, the emergence and current ubiquity of electronic media have had
a revolutionary influence on the nature of spaces of communication. Even today, the electronic and digital technologies continue to change the conditions
in which we relate and communicate with one another."(Van Berkel 07)

The "Thing" pavilion, designed and developed by UNStudio, divides space into two areas: one at the top of the installation for theater and drama; the other below, for art exhibition spaces. The theater is designed and constructed to provide an interactive space between the performer and the viewer. Observation points are informal and differ; providing interchangeable roles.
In contrast, at the New Amsterdam Plein & Pavilion in New York,     75, 76
programmatic functions are clearly delineated for information, refreshments and gathering. The design research for a form that offers a new city landmark is integrated with functional and communication requirements. It is situated within an organic and attractive complex that lends itself to multiple use and interpretation by either citizen or tourist. Digital technologies are employed at various stages of the design: The formal genesis is mainly carried out with three-dimensional modeling programs such as Rhino; often combined with Plug-In for the parametric design and scripting (Grasshopper). These multimedia installations are at the forefront of research in field of communication and are often solely linked to graphic design fields. The final phase of production is intertwined with new computerized construction techniques. The various components of these pavilions, typically built in a three-dimensional grid of wood framing and then covered with paneling and wall coverings, are computer-generated. The computerized ability to create three-dimensional molds or patterns for the cutting of the individual components makes it possible to execute these forms relatively quickly and with enormous precision. All the templates can be designed in Amsterdam and the components cut and assembled in New York rather than in Venice. The true re

THE THEATRE OF IMMANENCE, FRANKFURT ON THE RHINE, GERMANY, 2007
*Interiors photos*

plica between the virtual and the real model is guaranteed by the direct digital connection that exists between the two. The pavilion components are extracted directly from a three-dimensional computer model, with complete accuracy; without the conventional additional steps and filter that can lead to approximations and inaccuracies in the field.

In these small scale projects, UNStudio refines its mechanisms for creating, organizing and managing a project. This then makes it possible for them to create very complex buildings like the Mercedes Benz Museum or the Arnhem train station while, at the same time, continuing to research and experiment with formal and perceptual experiences that enrich their vocabulary and knowledge.

### 3.2 Façades and ornaments

The building skin is another fundamental area of research and experimentation in UNStudio's designs. By its very nature, a building façade acts as a filter between the inside and the outside of a project and defines an aesthetic and contextual impact on both city and user. At the same time, the technical, programmatic and climatic conditions make the design of the façade very exciting to a studio that is reaching for technological innovation. Once again UNStudio seeks to expand the concept of the facade, enriching it with new content and value.

The theme of the façade openings as well as its interaction within the urban context is re-interpreted. The building image is de-materialized and abstracted as much as possible to rework the many elements that have always made a building facade recognizable and identifiable. The window feature, in its traditional sense, almost disappears. Openings are placed in an organic manner within the formal and technical frameworks. The model incorporates three-dimensional geometry from its inception; integrating possible design changes with the functional and expressive components of the facade. Access points, openings, plan revisions and structure are not applied in a false manner to the envelope. These component requirements are defined at the start and often become the inspiration for new systems and expressions.

Their building decoration is developed as a stretched skin that increases the expressive qualities of a building and disappears. Ornament is construed as an abstract space. Baroque or Palladian de-

ANDREA SOLLAZZO

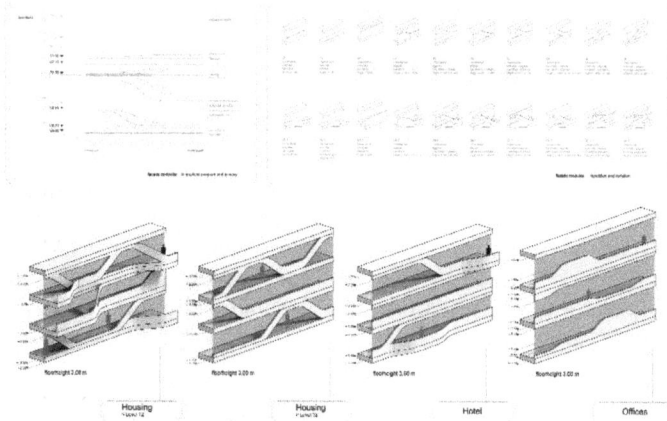

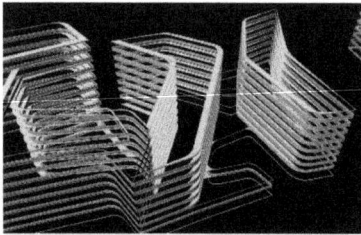

LIGHT HOUSE, AARHUS,
DENMARK, 2007

*Façade studies: interactivity
programs/forms the banding
"Horizontal bands wrapping the
buildings are transformed and
adapted to fit the different needs of
exposure, privacy and
programmatic functions. They also
establish a strong visual impact
while meeting excellent energy
performance and functional needs
of the facade."*

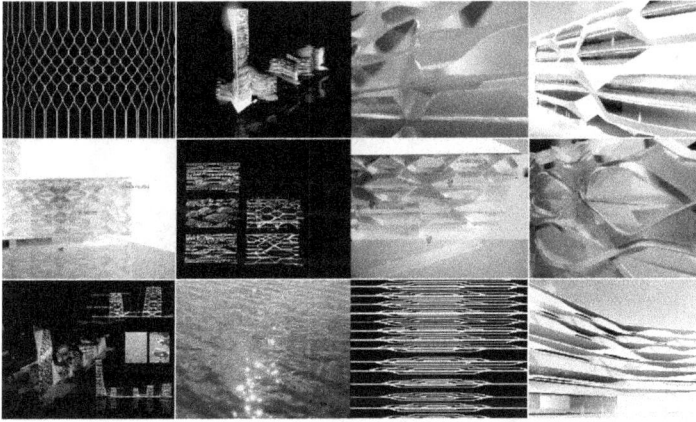

LIGHT HOUSE, AARHUS, DENMARK, 2007

*The end product is the result of constant iterations that mediate between formal, technical and functional needs. Above: Façade and research studies. Below: The final rendering.*

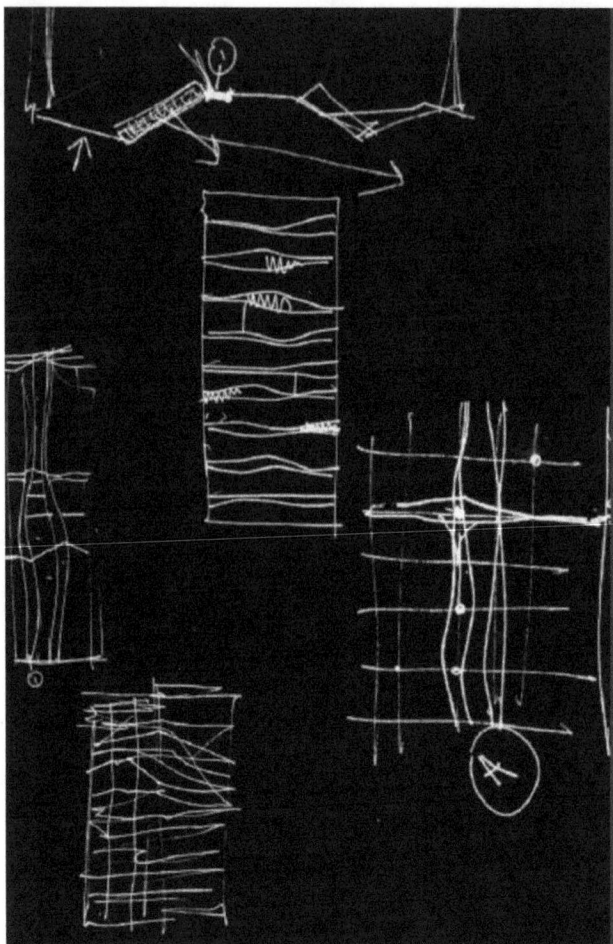

N. 5 FRANKLIN PLACE: NEW YORK, USA, 2007
*Study sketches for the deformation of the façade grid.*

coration, for example, was not simply ornamentation, but was the fruit and expression of the very geometric core of the design. This is an abstract idea more tied to a geometric reference than to a figurative aspect of the work, and in that manner it becomes the bearer of a message consistent with the formal and expressive matrix of the work. It is a subtle way to enrich the architectonic quality of communication. UNStudio strives to move in this direction;

"I like to reference back to Serlio, Palladio and any architects who were interested in mathematical geometrical constructs. [...] Through ornament they tried to emphasize the quality of an entrance or of a staircase and how all of this formed part of an abstract model. It was part of a greater whole even when it simply appeared to be decorative. I am interested in the idea of going from the rigid grid to soft organization and then back again, blob to box. I am most interested in the transition between the figurative and the abstract. Architecture is somewhere in the middle; not fully abstract nor fully figurative." (Van Berkel 09)

Technical and functional requirements are readily integrated into the decorative. Different lighting and ventilation needs become expressive features one with the façade. The transition from transparent to opaque surfaces, for example, is often achieved through a study of openings or screens within the stronger expressive theme. Needs become design opportunities and, once again, digital technology takes this beyond a virtual reality to a feasible and efficient construction.

Two clear examples of this approach are at Five Franklin Place, [82,84] (the Manhattan residential tower in New York), and Light *House, (a multifunctional complex of residences, offices and commercial services for the redevelopment of the port of Aarhus in Denmark). The building facades of these two projects, as often hap- [80,81] pens in the work of UNStudio, hold a common thread. The geometric and formal systems of both projects meet multiple expressive and functional needs. They succinctly encompass every aspect of the building front in a great single gesture that gives coherence and quality to the entire project.

Horizontal bands wrapping the buildings are transformed and [80,84] adapted to fit the different needs of exposure, privacy and programmatic functions. They also establish a strong visual impact while meeting excellent energy performance and functional needs of the facade. The building envelope is both continuous and chan-

**1** *Simple Twist*
+includes balconies
+various degrees of privacy

**2** *Shifted Twist*
+includes balconies
+various degrees of privacy
+bigger differentiation

**3** *Connected Twists*
+includes balconies
+various degrees of privacy
+larger appearance

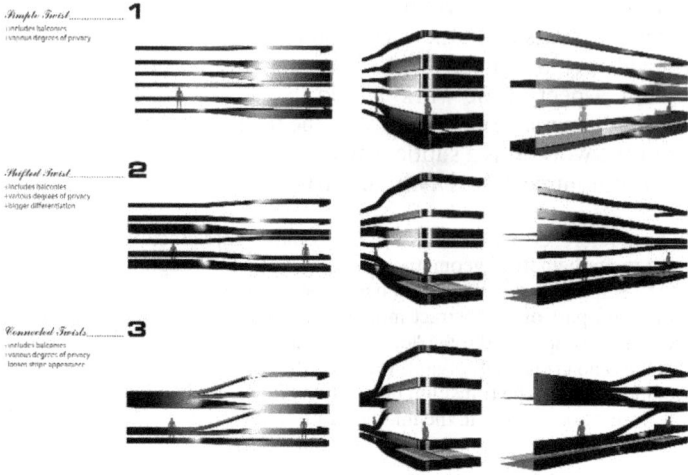

FIVE FRANKLIN PLACE: NEW YORK, USA, 2007

*Various system configurations of the horizontal banding that makes up the facade. The system is flexible and adapts to the different needs of the project without losing a formal coherence or becoming an accumulation of isolated incidents.*

ging. From the outside looking into the building, the façade offers a captivating, attractive and evocative image. From the inside out, however, the facade meets all functional and expressive small scale requirements of apartments, offices and shops. The horizontal bands act as screens to protect from excess of daylight, as balconies that protrude outside of the volume, as railings or infill, as framed views of the city or offer privacy to the dwelling from the outside world. The scale change from the city to the interior is through the invention and systematization of a formal and geometric system that integrates every aspect of the project. Just as in the Ponte Parodi, a set of specific potentials is defined to maximize function: a private residence has different needs from a public office or a restaurant. On this basis, a matrix of needs and potential is defined that regulates which bands change and adapt toward different configurations.

However, in public buildings such as theaters or museums, UNStudio's facade strategy defines openings and transitions from full to empty through the study of patterns and shapes. The facade is a literal membrane whose pores open and close as needed. Thanks to new design and construction technologies, such as laser cutters or 3D printers, they can quickly test and change templates with a high degree of accuracy.

Despite digital technology dramatically increasing design possibilities, it also introduces the risk of a sterile virtuosity that is detached from the original idea. Van Berkel and Bos maintain that technical knowledge and research will always require clarity of planning. If one takes for example the façade of the Dance Theatre of St. Petersburg, the openings get incrementally larger and frequent in relation to the public and performance spaces. The exterior envelope becomes lighter and bends at strategic points of the building; enhancing its quality and urban context. The facade design increases the abstract dimension of the building and creates a flowing and evocative body. The traditional articulation of planes disappears, the volume becomes a direct expression of the design concept and the distribution of openings becomes with the skin system. [34, 35]

Although it is not truly a façade, it is also interesting to analyze the envelope of UNStudio's competition entry for the extension of the Central Train Station of Bologna. The proposed envelope is original by typifying a parametric design approach. A single cell is de- [86]

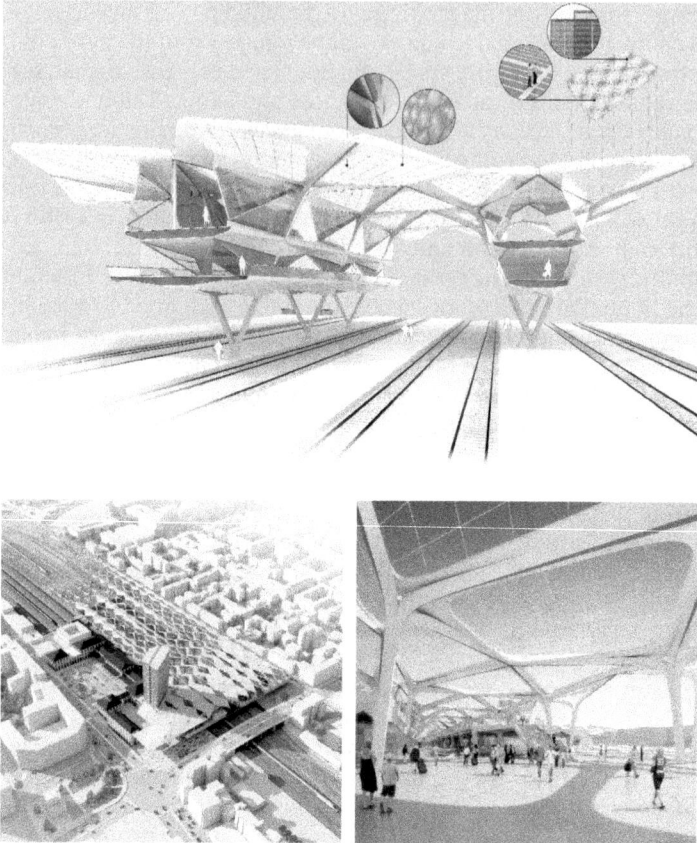

COMPETITION ENTRY FOR THE BOLOGNA MASTER PLAN AND TRAIN STATION, BOLOGNA, ITALY, 2007

*Above: A base cell. Each cell contains all the different needs: movement, texture, transparency or opacity to cover and install. This base unit can be repeated indefinitely and accumulated. Its innovation, compared to traditional modernist modular approach, is that the modules are not always the same, but flexible and adaptable to different design requirements. What are repeated are the system and the connections. The unit itself is transformable and a means for multiple and unrepeated solutions. Below: Aerial view and interior rendering.*

fined, a single feature and then, this feature undergoes several variations and mutations. The comparison to cell is very appropriate because, like a cell, this unit contains an internal DNA structure of information and connections, which guarantees its integrity, functionality and development. Thanks to its potential to connect and adapt, the cell can be repeated countless times and, under any necessary conditions, take on the required characteristics. It will provide full coverage where needed and will provide an open skeletal structure where coverage is not needed. This is a typical design characteristic for a parameter-based approach. Thanks to digital parameterized models one can design in every detail the base cell which can then be applied to the referenced surface; populating it. This is possible because what is planned and modeled is not a simple digital sculpture, but an intelligent three-dimensional model based on geometric, mathematical and structural functions. One can change scale, adapt and modify without ever changing the model's basic structure and internal relationships.

Obviously it is a methodology that requires a greater expenditure of time and effort in the preparation and organization of the digital base model. However, once a good model / system is developed, it provides for a tremendous increase in design possibilities with improved efficiency during implementation.

### 3.3 Soft interactivity

Interaction and communication in architectural design are typical of the digital age. Along with technological development that has brought new possibilities of expression, a society and culture has also developed that gives value to the transformability and adaptability of a product in an ever changing market and society. The concepts of interaction and product customization are now requisite and cornerstones of areas such as automotive, design, fashion, and the visual arts. The challenge in architecture becomes more [89,90] complicated: A building's interaction is never with a single user but must respond to multiple occupants. Transformation itself is a very complex and inefficient conceptual strategy when applied to large-scale buildings with a dominant building material. It is certainly easier to customize an iPod or a car and make it transform and adapt over time than to do this with a theater or a mall. However, the need for these built structures to adapt to quickly chan-

THEATRE AGORA,
LELYSTAD,
THE NETHERLANDS,
2007

*Façade panels and
patterning. The
shape and size of
different elevations
and panel units are
extracted directly
from the digital
model ensuring
total accuracy and
consistency between
the virtual model
and the construction
of the project.*

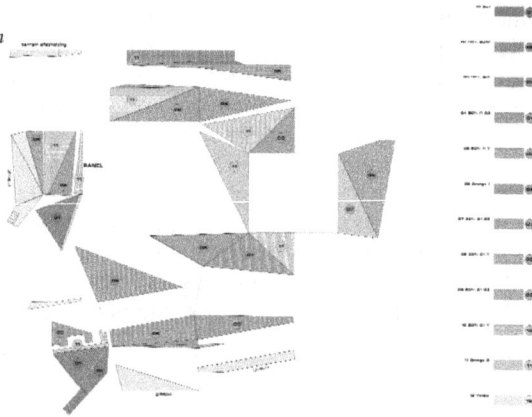

LA DEFENSE OFFICES, ALMERE, THE NETHERLANDS, 2004

STAR PALACE, FACADE, KAOHSIUNG, TAIWAN, 2006-2008

*"The building is de-materialized, with a constantly changing picture that can vary from abstract visual effects to advertisements; making the mall not only a container of goods but itself an interactive tool of communication."*

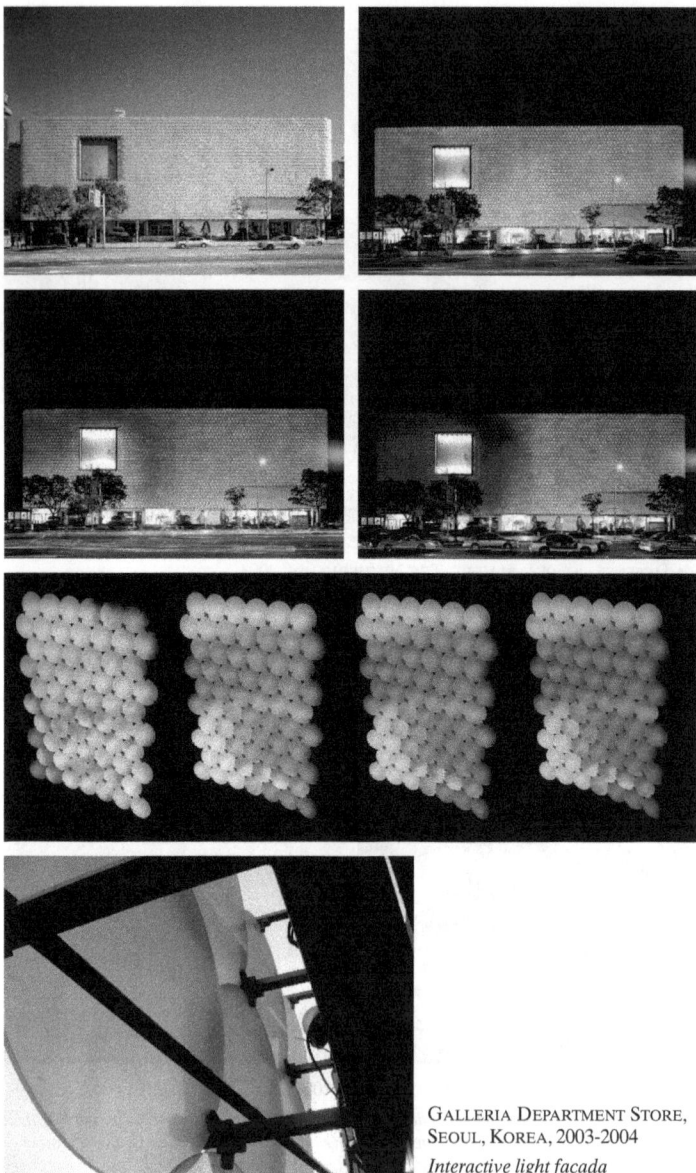

GALLERIA DEPARTMENT STORE,
SEOUL, KOREA, 2003-2004
*Interactive light facada*

ging economic, social and cultural environment is as necessary today. Their adaptability affects their efficiency value and determines their essential quality of interaction. An image of an attractive and innovative building greatly increases its productive capacity in the eyes of both the market and the average citizen. The ability to integrate within an architectural facade interactive features that are transformable is an opportunity offered by the new technological developments that UNStudio employs. They do not focus on the direct interaction between the building and the citizen, but rather on the interaction between the building and the client or between the building and the environment; both as physical context and as a space for communication. In several projects, the facade becomes an actual illuminated billboard that can display graphics and color. The façade becomes a light source, a picture and a pixel. Different types of lighting or color can be digitally programmed as needed. Even in this case, the digital decoration is not reduced to a simple screen attached to the surface of the building, but the skin itself is the actual screen. UNStudio studies façade systems for each project that fully incorporate the feature within the base skin of the building. This feature may be the pixel unit that will then define the greater facade. They seek a design solution that Van Berkel and Bos define as the "inclusive principle" that succeeds in a single gesture and with a single system in incorporating all levels of complexity that a project requires.

A very interesting example of this interaction and communication, among many, is their design for a commercial center in Seoul, Korea. UNStudio was asked to renovate the facade and the interior of a large shopping mall, the Galleria Hall West. Their design concept for the facade provides an enclosure for the building that adapts itself to the changing world of fashion, the different seasons and can continuously reinvent itself, change and interact with new trends and commercial and communication needs. The facade consists of 4.330 frosted glass circular disks attached to the building structure; each of which is illuminated by three digitally controlled LEDs. The discs are like pixels on a screen that can create different effects and images. Through this feature, the building is de-materialized, with a constantly changing picture that can vary from abstract visual effects to advertisements; making the mall not only a container of goods but itself an interactive tool of communication.

UNStudio research and application of interactivity also extends to
an "environmental" façade that interacts with external environmental components, with adjacent colors, and with the landscape
and nature surrounding the project. The façade not only reflects,
but interprets and transforms the world around it. Searching for
materials and techniques that can give this result led UNStudio to
develop several projects where the environmental component of
interaction enhanced the designs in new and unexpected ways.
Two projects exemplary of this process are the Agora Theatre in
Lelystad and the office building of La Defense in Almere.

88   Albeit in a different way, the two buildings interact with both the
environment and the human eye. A kaleidoscopic effect is given to
the Agora Theatre by the various plane changes in the faceted volume which comprises the building. The design is enhanced by a
facade treatment that provides for the overlapping of different levels of screening with different patterns of openings. Depending
on the angle and the eye and incidence of light, this reveals an ever
changing chromatic effect.

A similar effect, but employing a different technique, is also found
89   in the La Defense office building. Here the treatment of the facade contributes even more strongly to the de-materialization of the
building volume. It creates a new world derived from the surrounding environment, and brings forth new ideas and interpretations.
The facade overlooking the courtyard of the office building is coa-
ted with a film that changes color depending on light and point of
view; changing from blue to red to yellow. These chromatic effects
and reflections are so intense as to color not only the facade of the
building but they spread upon the pavement and the whole interior court; offering visitors a new and heightened sensory experience.

# Glossary

**Desing Models:** Van Berkel and Bos define these as "principles of organization and composition, enhanced by the construction parameters."

**Inclusive Principle:** a base model, one that encompasses all the others. It opposes postmodernist fragmentation and collage. The principle highlights the need for a synthesized response that does not isolate the different aspects of architectural design, but instead looks for a merging and interrelations between differences.

**Mathematical Model:** a geometric reference model, which is regulated by a particular mathematical order such as the Möbius strip or Klein bottle.

**Blob-to-box Model:** a system in which an organizational transformation is possible based on a fluid and open element moving toward a rigid and closed one.

**V Model:** begins as a structural model to create continuity within a vertical space. It is enhanced over time to become a real three-dimensional organizational model.

**Deep Planning Principle:** is a method of analysis, study and design on an urban scale that analyzes the city not only in its apparent forms and exterior, but tries to understand the forces, flows and dynamics that animate it.

**Mobil Forces:** are a method of study and analysis of the city or a particular site that is focused on dynamic factors such as time, people and circulation.

**Parametric Design:** a design method that organizes the project into a three-dimensional model in which elements are described via mathematical equations that allow compatible changes to the project components.

**Hierarchical Model:** a system based on differentiating between a primary object and an instance. The object contains all required geometrical data. The instance, (also known as an Alias, Block, or Symbol in specific digital applications), reads the object's geometrical data and then locates, deforms and replicates the object multiple times in space. A hierarchical model organizes a project through an inverted pyramid of relationships. This model allows for a global scale tracking of any change to the primary object (geometric, cost, physical characteristics) and it is automatically relayed to all possible instances. It is a very powerful tool when combined with parametric design to become what is commonly identified as BIM or Building Information Modeling (Saggio, 2007).

# Bibliography

Van Berkel 09 - *Conversation between Andrea Sollazzo and Ben van Berkel*, UNStudio, Amsterdam July 2009.

Van Berkel, Bos 02 - Ben van Berkel, Caroline Bos, *UN Studio, UNFOLD*, Nai Publishers, Rotterdam 2002.

Betsky 02 - Ben van Berkel, Caroline Bos, *UN Studio, UNFOLD*, Nai Publisher, Rotterdam 2002.

Van Berkel, Bos 08 - Ben van Berkel, Caroline Bos, *Move*, UN Studio & Goose Press 2008.

Bos 95, Ben Van Berkel 1990-1995 *El Croquis*, n. 72 1995, El Croquis Editorial, Madrid 1995.

Lynn 95, Grez Lynn, "Ben Van Berkel 1990-1995", *El Croquis*, n. 72 1995, El Croquis Editorial, Madrid 1995.

Van Berkel, Bos 06 - Ben van Berkel, Caroline Bos, *Model*, Thames and Hudson Ltd. London 2006.

Van Berkel 07 - Ben Van Berkel, *Installation brochure publication for The theatre of immanence - Portikus*, Frankfurt, 2007.

Van Berkel 06 - Ben Van Berkel, Caroline Bos, *Buy Me a Mercedes Benz: The Book of the Museum*, Actar Barcelona 2006.

Saggio 07 - Antonino Saggio - *Introduzione alla rivoluzione informatica in architettura*, Carrocci Editore, Rome 2007.

McCullough 05 - Malcolm McCullough, *Digital ground*, MIT Press paperback edition, Cambridge, Massachusetts 2005.

Laura Negrini - *Ben Van Berkel*, Edilstampa, Rome 2001.

Ali Rahim - *Catalytic Formation Architecture and digital design*, Taylor & Francis, Oxon 2006.

AD 02 - "Contemporary Techniques in Architecture", *Architectural Design* vol.72 No1 Jan. 2002.

AD 04 - "Emergence: Morphogenetic Design Strategies", *Architectural Design* vol. 74 No3 May/June 2004.

Marotta 04 - Antonello Marotta, *Ben Van Berkel, la prospettiva rovesciata di UNStudio*, Testo &Immagine, Rome 2004.

Barzon 03, Frurio Barzon, *La carta di Zurigo*, Eisenman, De Kerckhove Saggio, Testo&Immagine, Rome 2003.

Rem Koolhaas, *Delirious New York a Retroactive Manifesto for Manhattan*, Monacelli Press New York 1997 (first ed. 1978).


*Internet Sources*

http://www.unstudio.com/
http://www.wenzel-wenzel.de/
http://www.designtoproduction.ch/index.php
http://www.boll-und-partner.de
http://www.fivefranklinplace.com/#/1
http://www.arnhemcentraal.nu/
http://www.bloemendaalendekkers.nl/index2.html

# Contents

Digital Sustainability                                                    5
*Introduction by Antonino Saggio*


1. Organizational qualities of architecture                              9
*1.1 Data*                                                               15
*1.2 The calm after the storm: a bazaar of forms*                       20


2. Principals for digital design and computer architecture              24
*2.1 Design Models: dynamic and transformable models*                   24
*2.2 The design model is the tool, but never the design itself*         28
*2.3 Digital thinking*                                                   36
*2.4 Rubber Mat*                                                         37
*2.5 The expansion of the line*                                         41
*2.6 Project development: sustainable digital design*                    46
*2.7 The programmatic dimension*                                        55
*2.8 Ponte Parodi, continuous and endless organization*                 59


3. Form, fluidity and soft interactivity                                68
*3.1 Installations and small worlds*                                    72
*3.2 Façades and ornaments*                                             79
*3.3 Soft interactivity*                                                87


Glossary                                                                93


Bibliography                                                            94

*The Information Technology Revolution in Architecture* is a series reflecting on the effects the virtual dimension is having on architects and architecture in general. Each volume will examine a single topic, highlighting the essential aspects and exploring their relevance for the architects of today.

Other titles in this series

**Diller + Scofidio**
Il teatro
della dissolvenza
Antonello Marotta
ISBN 88-7864-010-7 *Italiano*
    978-1-4466-7679-0 *Inglese*

**Gamezone**
Playground tra scenari virtuali
e realtà
Alberto Iacovoni
ISBN 88-7864-011-5

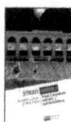

**Strati Mobili**
Video contestuali
nell'arte e nell'architettura
Alexandro Ladaga & Silvia Manteiga
ISBN 88-7864-016-6

**Takis Zenetos**
Visioni digitali,
architetture costruite
Dimitris Papalexopoulos, Eleni Kalafati
ISBN 88-7864-012-3

**Arie italiane**
Motivi dell'architettura
italiana recente
Antonello Marotta, Paola Ruotolo
ISBN 88-7864-022-0

**Stanze ribelli**
Immaginando
lo spazio hacker
Alexander Levi, Amanda Schachter
ISBN 978-88-7864-028-3

**Penezic & Rogina**
Digitalizzazione
della realtà
Nigel Whiteley
ISBN 978-88-7864-030-6 *Italiano*
    978-1-4461-0015-8 *Inglese*

**Ipercorpi**
Verso una
architettura e-motiva
Kas Oosterhuis
ISBN 978-88-7864-037-5

**Ito digitale**
Nuovi media,
nuovo reale
Patrizia Mello
ISBN 978-88-7864-044-3

**SHoP Works**
Collaborazioni costruttive
in digitale
Stefano Converso
ISBN 978-88-7864-045-0 *Italiano*
    978-1-4478-4748-9 *Inglese*

**Cyberstone**
Innovazioni digitali
sulla pietra
Christian R. Pongratz, M. Rita Perbellini
ISBN 978-88-7864-051-4

**La forma come memoria**
Una teoria geometrica
dell'architettura
Michael Leyton
ISBN 978-88-7864-055-9

**Van Berkel digitale**
Diagrammi, processi, modelli
di UNStudio
Andrea Sollazzo
ISBN 978-88-7864-070-2 *Italiano*
    978-1-4478-6706-7 *Inglese*

www.ingramcontent.com/pod-product-compliance
Lightning Source LLC
Chambersburg PA
CBHW060132050426
42448CB00010B/2086